HIGH ENDEAVORS

By Pat Ament

"Man, if he do but live within the light of high endeavors, daily spreads abroad his being with a strength that cannot fail." —
Wordsworth

Published by Mountain N' Air Books

Table of Contents

Evocation

John Ciardi writes, "Let what I love outlive me and all's well." And, "I have no worlds to change and none to keep." Our ideas see with emotion, fail at their expectations, and after all the change our lives seem to bring to a terrain the terrain drifts ultimately back to itself. Life darkens sometimes, like the rock, however momentarily luminous a day may turn the rock and us. Cracks drip, and sun is on ancient, mysterious ledges. An afternoon before the sun leaves the east face of Longs Peak (the spelling without the possessive has become convention), a climbing route approaches through the air. Resistance from lungs, legs, minds, clouds in attires of consummation, eminently white, circular, forming corridors upward into sky. Granite forms in the cores of mountains— geology. But put that in the context of Longs Peak. The east face is vertical for two thousand feet, sheer in its top thousand—called the Diamond. The shell of the mountain is missing, fallen away, exposing what's inside, although it now too is falling. A block the size of a bus flew past my head one day while climbing. Normally the movement is in pebbles and in aeons. Sun, air, starlight chip at the rock, rock that pays no mind to a college degree or to how long it takes to earn a woman's affections, yet such things are there, can be seen, in the starlight, in the stone—yellow, gray, brown, sometimes red as cedar, falling.

Love forms in the cores of people. Sun, starlight chip at the outer shell. We give these ascents to each other. We share these experiences so that when we see a certain rock, or a mountain, we see each other, we remember. Climbing is a wide, general thought that you develop and where you feel what you are worth—a few explicit, solid holds, and a few other holds that have a terror to them, looking always for the route, for the will to look and to continue, amid probables of weather. There is a strong feeling to ascending rock. You place the feet with precision on tiny deceptions, press the texture of your fingertips into attitudes. You more or less master this process but remain year after year intrigued by it as it unfolds in endless new ways. You merge with the sun and alpine flowers and yourself, store thoughts of the persons you go with. The exposure makes you feel the sanctuary of your strength together.

A step loosens a stone. The world attempts to retrail itself. Water falls over a slab. Ptarmigan walk alongside you in the tundra. You sketch poetry in your mind, images which are the references of your specific internal terrain and which bear all of the finest or most disturbing, secret clarity and deepnesses of breath. This is fragrant breathing. Cold, beautiful, flyable, ptarmigan air.

Trail walkers far above seem to taunt you as inferior. They form a type of procession as though content to migrate toward some distant colony. They started as first investigators from the mire and now inhabit the end of time. It is easy to lose heart in growing weather and with impending distances. Altitude works a fine sensitivity toward feminine expression, a study so strong that no trail is needed, only light coming, going, and maneuvers of clouds. A few drops of rain tap on the shoulders of your jacket. Somehow a mountain, or rock, stands before you in the form of your happiness or your sorrow, again returning to you with its wind that blows across blank, gray rock. You feel the space of your life shrink as your understanding expands. You try to call back whatever you can of adolescence, for example when you climbed the Diamond as a highschool senior, the wall's fourth ascent, when the wall was more fearsome but you were less fearful, stages of early, unannounced life where suddenly you were who you were, a climber, and there was a vague line between the true and the imagined, celebrated as joy.

For a moment a madness attacks your thoughts. Somehow you need madness and death as you need sanity and climbing. You never leave such things. They lunge at you from your memories, and from your dreams, nights as you look down from ledges or up at galaxies or as you walk over the crackly sand of a trail, upward some crowning morning, writing in your thoughts, a hope to mend some of the sorrows, to reclaim a few sunlights and joys lost with time, futilely. But that is another one of those important emotions, to explore systematically what you may never remember, a challenging, provisional terrain. And then night places a veil of carbon once more over the Diamond.

— Pat Ament November 1990

No one was fully adequate to the difficulties of climbing with Layton Kor, but the following story portrays me at my worst. The story was published first in Mountain Magazine, in 1976, also in a publication called Colorado High Country, and then by Ken Wilson in The Games Climbers Play, an international collection of best climbing writings (1978), published in England. The article was chosen again in 1988 for a European anthology of best climbing writings, published in Germany, edited by Nicholas Mailander, and called Poeten Des Abgrunds.

When it first came out, the article caused chaos. People either found it hilarious or thought it heretical. A few who idolized Kor resented my descriptions of both his physical person and his character. I never intended to be derogatory. The events of the story are really very factual, as accurate as possible through the eyes of one as impressionable as I was at the time, yet it is a story that inclines toward caricature — Kor's inimicable best. Whereas in his autobiography he somewhat idealizes himself, Kor was in the '60s compulsive, downright dangerous upon occasion, and — more often than he might admit — concerned chiefly with his personal ambitions. At the same time, no one more appreciates Kor, or appreciated Kor at that time, than I. His greatness, the joy of being with him — indisputable.

The Black Canyon With Kor

"I...let myself down rapidly, striving by the vigor of my movements to banish the trepidation which I could overcome in no other manner.... But presently I found my imagination growing terribly excited by thoughts of the vast depths yet to be descended.... It was in vain I endeavored to banish these reflections and to keep my eyes steadily bent upon the flat surface of the cliff before me. The more earnestly I struggled not to think, the more intensely vivid became my conceptions, and the more horribly distinct. At length arrived that crisis of fancy, so fearful in all similar cases, the crisis

in which we begin to anticipate the feelings with which we shall fall - to picture to ourselves the sickness, and dizziness, and the last struggle, and the half swoon, and the final bitterness of the rushing and headlong descent. And now I found these fancies creating their own realities, and all imagined horrors crowding upon me in fact. I felt my knees strike violently together, while my fingers were gradually but certainly relaxing their grasp. And now I was consumed with the irrepressible desire of looking below. I could not, I would not, confine my glances to the cliff; and, with a wild indefinable emotion, half of horror, half of a relieved oppression, I threw my vision far down into the abyss. For one moment my fingers clutched convulsively upon their hold, while, with the movement, the faintest possible idea of ultimate escape wandered, like a shadow, through my mind - in the next my whole soul was pervaded with a longing to fall...." - Edgar Allan Poe

This passage of Poe's from his tale of Arthur Gordon Pym, brings to mind certain feelings which I had the misfortune - or fortune - to experience in Colorado's Black Canyon of the Gunnison at age seventeen under the unique guidance of Layton Kor, my climbing partner, who at that time was twenty-five. An extraordinary, absurd, humorous, stupid, and altogether dangerous ordeal took place.

Layton had recovered instantaneously from an unbelievable, backwards, head-over-heels leader fall off the Bastille Crack in Eldorado. My hands, however, were blistered nearly shut from the serious rope burns I suffered catching him. I had been warned by a doctor to stay away from rock for at least a month, as the blisters were in danger of becoming infected, but Layton was impatient and wanted to depart immediately for the Black Canyon. He showed me a fuzzy snapshot of a 2000ft., vertical and overhanging wall called The Chasm View and reassured me that I was tough. I wanted to be with him, and Layton's wide eyes and warm laugh were persuasive. Just the thought of such a first ascent was enough to take my mind off the burns and diminish, in my idiocy and immaturity, all pain.

It was the middle of summer, and the three hundred or so mile drive from Boulder was hot. The old, blue Ford had four bald tires, and Kor gunned it up to eighty miles-an-hour most of the way. His eyes bulged and face contorted as he drove. His huge form leaned over the steering wheel, and he gazed nervously ahead. He held a peanut butter sandwich between his long legs and knobby knees and shook to the tune of rock 'n' roll which blasted out of the radio. I sat gripping the seat, making peanut butter sandwiches at Kor's command and, at one point, agreeing to take part in a handshake contest. There were two hundred pounds backing up his grip and about a hundred and thirty behind mine. My blisters burned at the thought, and I was squeezed out like a flame. A poor little chipmunk was flattened while attempting to cross the highway.

The final part of the drive was a fifty-mile dirt road above cliffs and steep drops which were the beginning of the Black Canyon. I was terrorized by this road, its unending, sharp curves, and the drag racer behind the wheel. A lump of laughter and peanut butter stayed in my mouth for what seemed like an hour.

We arrived at the north rim of the canyon late in the day, parked, and after a brief walk were able to peer down our wall. The eerie, distant roar of the Gunnison River which flowed far below, combined with the peculiar, lonely fragrance of sage, the desert-like silence, and hot wind, began to stir in me a fear of the remote area. My heart sank at the thought of having to catch another Kor fall or of encountering one of the huge, horribly rotten, sickly pink, pegmatite bands which Layton had, during the drive, described with dread and superstition.

Layton snatched me up into his arms, pretending to have gone mad and to want to throw me over the edge. His fun was soon over, for I shot away from the exposed place like a rabbit, desperate to escape his chuckles. I endeavored to console myself, returned, and was from then on prepared to bear with personality and fortitude all further absurdity which was destined to occur.

After briefly exploring a steep, alien gully which appeared to be a feasible descent route into the canyon, we spent a bad night on the rim. It was anticipation of the climb that kept us awake, also hunger. We had practically depleted our supply of bivouac food- the peanut butter - and would have been foolish to break into the small ration of meat which Layton had brought in addition. Kor was immensely energetic and would not be discouraged by heat or hunger. Thinking to stimulate me in the morning with a cup of boiling tea, he exploded his small stove and nearly burned down a picnic table. This put him in a bad humor, and he stared at me with a look as insidious as a sly sun which rose and began drawing the first beads of sweat from my forehead. We sorted pitons, slings, and carabiners, loaded bivouac gear into a large haul bag, filled a couple of water bottles, stuffed bolts and provisions into an old pack, and headed off to descend the steep gully.

My thoughts were with facing the fear, with moving into Layton's world. I needed to discover life, to help find this route, and, if necessary, be led blindly by the master. The descent was hideous! The sultry gully into the canyon was filled with soil and sticker bushes. Small whimpers in a fretful, broken voice were my sound of protest. Proceeding down into the expanse of the gully, we found it suffocating. It was a treacherous sort of chute, eventually becoming slippery walls on all sides. Layton had loaded onto me what seemed an enormous amount of rope and hardware - plus the old pack. It was not easy to breathe with slings choking me and pack straps tearing at my shoulders. It felt unfair.

The heat was unbearable. An hour into the morning, I was ready to consume our entire two-day supply of water in a sitting. I was anxious, watching Kor descend without a belay. He moved smoothly down the precipitous, slabby walls of the gully. The weight upon my shoulders and around my neck made it impossible to follow without great strain. At one difficult section, a tiny slip would have meant a fall of about 800ft. This took a lot out of me, and I worked up a horrible sweat. My burned hands stung as they scraped across crystals. I listened to the river crash over boulders below, and the sound slashed at my thoughts. I groped at loose flakes, contemplating the anguish of one coming off in my hand. I wanted to do well, to win respect, to cling successfully to Kor's dream. My muscles quivered, and the moves were hazy before my eyes. Layton lowered himself down bulges, over ledges, and around bizarre heaps of gravel. He descended confidently, having no trouble with his load and ignoring my struggles. He was full of hope. I was a scorpion.

Layton was for a moment thirsty but could not relax for thinking about getting to the base of the route. He carried the bottles of water in the haul bag, and I prayed that he would save a sip. I licked the parched lining of my mouth. Who was this maniac? Why was I permitting myself to go along with him?

At last, we were at the base of the route, dripping with sweat and trying to solve the puzzle of rope and snarl of slings which bound me. My hands were soft and white, oozing with pus which drained from a couple of broken blisters. Kor allowed me a swallow or two of water, which only antagonised my thirst, then tied-in and led upward. A towering illusion, tall as a man, with white T-shirt and pants, long socks, and klettershoe, hung on an overhang above my head. The jeweled light of the sun scorched my thoughts. I had, above me, a kind of surrealism - a creature whose ability on rock matched my vision - Layton Kor, spread eagled and silhouetted, his senses suspended momentarily but bodily powers frenzied. I squeezed the rope, then fed it out as he led swiftly up a difficult crack. The man was driven, afraid to fall, afraid to fail, tormented, all-powerful in a search for rich experience. He ascended with imagination, inclined to go the hard way when a choice existed, tense, uneasy, jumpy, jittery, happy. He was awesome - more so than the wall - and disappeared into the lair of an overhang. I sat like a piece of cactus, sweltering, stifled in a furnace of talus, awaiting the restless cry, "Come on up!" The river was a hundred-and-fifty yards below and glistened even in the shadows. Scrambling down to it for a cold drink was an idea dismissed in view of the uphill hike back.

He was too big for belay ledges and looked uncomfortable hooked into one. As I followed the pitch, attacking strenuous pulls and long reaches, I discovered that my worst opponent was the old pack. While thinking I was in perfect balance, I would start to fall backwards and would expend precious energy recovering. My hands were a mess, and it was difficult even to hold a piton hammer - much less pound out pins. I was unable to retrieve the first piton, although I worked at it to the point of exhaustion. I was convinced that Layton had over-driven the thing and so left it. I began to feel extremely insecure and yelled for tension. I received slack. The lack of communication was frustrating, and my yells were overruled by the superior authority of the river. When I reached Layton, he asked, "You get that pin out?" I trembled and replied, "I have it here somewhere." He complained of aching feet and insisted on doing the next lead. I was too busy contemplating my lie to argue, so belayed. He stemmed over an impressive overhang and vanished into the heights. The route seemed to have been built for Kor, because I found the holds always out of reach. Layton suggested I take the third lead. It was incentive to forget for awhile the sorry state of my palms. The hammer was too painful to hold, but the rock relented momentarily, so I was able to climb unprotected to a stance about 100ft. straight up. Kor was impressed with this but irritated when I could not haul the bag. My hands simply couldn't take it. He hurried up the pitch, and we tugged at the clumsy duffel bag together. That was the end of my leading, I was informed.

It was at this point that war began. Suddenly and quite unexpectedly, Kor yelled, "Where's your hard hat?!" I answered, "My what?" He thrust a handful of rope against the wall with such force that I thought we would both fall off. He kicked the wall and, looking as if he was going to strangle me, shouted, "No one climbs in the Black Canyon without a hard hat!" I was so intimidated by this outburst that I failed to notice he was not wearing one either. I indiscreetly let pass, at this moment, a bit of silent although untimely "flatus" of so foul and putrid an odor that all oxygen was removed from the vicinity of our perch. It took but an instant (which seemed an eternity) for the very bad message to reach Kor's nose. Now I almost unroped with the intention of jumping rather than face the frightful demon who stood gagging so near at hand. He hovered over me, his face puffing with rage. He let out a chilling scream and raced up the wall, not bothering to place pitons where he knew I would need them. I nearly vomited when he thrust himself into a ferocious, dizzy, overhanging crack and forced his way up it with rope and haul-line dangling down to me like cobras.

All flexibility had gone out of my fingers. I removed the pack and set it atop the haul bag which sat comfortably on the stance without an anchor. It was surely a hundred degrees out, and my thirst was intolerable. I forced a hand and arm into the bag and pulled out a bottle. While belaying with one hand, I twisted the top off with my teeth and began to guzzle. The tone of the climb had changed so radically that I felt faint. A muted "off belay" from above told me that I had best get the bottle back into the bag fast. Stealing water might be punished by more unprotected leading. As I fumbled with the bottle and bag, the haul line grew tight, and, just as the bottle disappeared into the opening, up went the big bag with my pack teetering, to my horror and dismay, on top where I had set it. The heavy bundle remained intact and was dragged over a bulge and up into a place hidden from my view where, by all indications, Kor was losing his mind with anger. "Oh my God, my arms are numb," he raved.

I had to keep my wits about me. A display of skill, I thought, might save me from the wrath of the fiend above. But it was all I could do to gain an inch on the pitch without tension. I very skillfully wore my voice out bellowing for the tight line. My hands were two blobs of dirt, pus, and shredded skin.

At the belay, he had regained his composure but did not speak to me. We hung from slings attached to two feebly-placed knifeblade pitons which Layton was eager to get away from. A severe chimney became the object of his study. He would climb it conscientiously, I reasoned, for there was no desire to die here...was there? I was delirious and needed water. Adrenalin flowed, and as I found myself somehow following the obstacle - the 5.10 crack-chimney affair - I was bewildered and inspired by techniques which I applied but did not understand. There are expressions of struggle that are deeply found. I became confused, drew upon untapped resources, and stretched my limbs through a hundred variations of divine bumbling. "Heel and toe," Kor shrieked. I was encouraged, but slipped several feet down, trying to figure out what he meant. One thing for sure: the pack and I would not both fit into the slot at once. Kor advised me to try the "Yosemite haul." I was to hook the pack to a long sling, then the sling to my waist loop, and drag the pack as it hung well below. I regretted tackling such a scheme, for it was 5.11 just getting the beast off my back. Then the buckles of the straps caught on every conceivable projection until I was certain that the tension from above and immovable weight below would tear me in half.

I somehow achieved Kor's position, after pulling and being hauled on the rope. Kor did not delay in leading up one more unbelievable, overhanging, obscure pitch. His tremendous skill was evident. It was easy to know why he was one of the great climbers of the world.

The pitch was all direct aid, and (jumar prusik handles having not yet been invented) I thought I would die trying to reach from one carabiner to the next. As usual, Layton could not see me and was unable to determine whether my winded gripes were from falling, trying to get tension, or just pain. I would give each piton a half-hearted tap and grimace, before deciding that it was over-driven and a permanent fixture. I had no hands left, no voice, no spirit, only hope that we could bivouac, drink the water, and somehow rejuvenate. All the pitons stayed in, and I was ashamed but kept fighting.

As I drained the last of my will trying to surmount the belay ledge, I caught sight of my companion. Kor's hair pointed in every direction. His mouth and eyes were full of dirt. Sweat rolled down his cheeks. His famous buck teeth were the focus of an inimitable grin. He was a rebel with a bit of a temper, supremely talented, fueled by sheer force, set off from other climbers by a light - an illumination or charisma - and profound competence. He asked, "Did you get all the pins?" I had none with me but seemed to feel that the summit was near and that a few of the little iron strips would not be missed. I was unable to speak but simply nodded my head in the affirmative while reclining and gasping for air. We were seven hundred or more feet above the gully, a little less than half way to the rim. Kor gave me a worried glance and observed, "You look bad, Ament. You're pale." He then ventured up onto the next formidable pitch, examining it for its qualities.

What was I to do or say? I regarded life at that instant as an illness for which help was not available. I dreaded the thought of continuing but also feared retreat. Going down would mean Kor finding the pitons still in place. It would mean having to thrash our way back up the horrible gully. To my amazement Kor returned and, with no explanation, made preparations for rappelling. It was only later that I would feel it was Kor's genuine concern for my condition which turned him back. He placed a bolt, and I watched the small thing bend in its hole as he applied his weight to the rope. I listened to the tinging of metal against metal as he discovered and removed the pitons I'd left. Small, indistinct curses drifted up to me and, finally, "Off rappel." I was sure that I would not be able to hold onto the rope - even with a break bar - but resigned myself to try. Layton kept guard over the rope ends, in case I decided to pick up speed. In the course of the rappel, my blisters became mangled cuts.

Kor detested my lack of candor about the pitons, and so did I. That was half the hurt. His smiles gnawed at me with excruciating clarity. For an instant he was understanding, and I remembered other sides of him which existed - patient, insightful sides. My wretchedness and misery permeated the desolation of his stare, and my dejected state brought upon Kor an eagerness to escape the Black Canyon of the Gunnison and all of southwestern Colorado.

A quick, violent rainstorm gave us relief but was accompanied by several disturbing bolts of lightning and thunder crashes. After several agonizing rappels, we stood at the bottom in darkness. The ominous, forbidding, evil gully rose endlessly above. Kor withdrew upwards into the night, leaving me to the demons, as well as with a rack of hardware and heavy, rain-drenched rope which I could barely lift. I had let my heart be molded by him and, strangely, knew that I would probably do so again. I loved Kor and hated him and in no way could deny either. The gully was a horrid task, and I was alone in it. Kor was somewhere far ahead, maybe almost up to the rim, possibly in pieces below.

I persevered toward a glimmer of sky, up steep slabs, through mud and stickers, over loose boulders, as if steering my bones through the grave, and clawing in the direction of a dim glow - the headlights of the Ford. My exertions became greater. I stumbled through sage, got into the car, shut the door, and fell asleep. Layton was determined to grind-out the drive back to Boulder that night.

I wished not to awaken out of my dream and into the nightmare of his speeding along the scary, dirt road. He was sailing around corners in the wrong lane and demanding that I sing songs to keep him awake. There was only static on the radio. I groaned a few hoarse and sour notes while leaning slowly over onto his nervous lap, falling back to sleep. He tried to wake me several times, and I would sit up, only to slide rigidly back over onto his lap like a corpse, still dutifully humming.

My eyes opened in the town of Gunnison. It was past midnight, we had stopped, and Kor stood outside rapping on the door of an A. & W. Rootbeer stand which was closed. He looked like death and for all practical purposes frightened the janitor into letting him in. The fellow was obliged to fix the apparition a float! I went back to sleep. Was it really happening?

About an hour later, Layton pulled off onto what appeared to be a turn-out, stopped, got out of the car, and threw his sleeping-bag, me, and my sleeping-bag into the dirt. There we slept for the rest of the night. At the crack of dawn, we made a quick dash to the Ford, delivering ourselves from a rancher's perverse sense of humor and two thousand hooves of five hundred cows being herded toward us.

Kor said nothing to me all the way home but, upon arriving in Boulder, reported to a number of other climbers. His account of the ordeal was marked by a lack of particulars and was, simply, "Ament...left all the pins in, so we had to come back." I recalled saving his life on the Bastille Crack in Eldorado and felt that he was being ungrateful. I began to realize how hard I had actually pushed on the wall of the Chasm View and in the exposed gully. Through young eyes and foolish insecurity, I saw Layton as the dishonest one... but, with a bit of reflection, returned to my senses. He had told the truth, really. I understood and forgave him for his madness. He had shown me the Black Canyon, perplexed me, tortured my will and ego. But following our adventure, he made plans to climb with me again in Eldorado, forgot for awhile about the Chasm View, laughed, and, after all, was my friend.

Layton Kor on "The Rupper Traverse," Eldorado Springs 1962
Photo by Charles Roskosz

Climbing with Royal Robbins on Longs Peak, in the deserts of Utah and New Mexico, in Salt Lake City, Yosemite, Tuolumne, Boulder Canyon, and Eldorado was among the best, most memorable, and most instructive experience of my life. The following story of my first encounter with him in 1964 appeared originally in Climbing Magazine, April 1980, and then in Mirrors in The Cliffs (1983), an international anthology of best climbing writings compiled by Jim Perrin and published in England.

It meant a lot to me when, in the winter of 1987 at an American Alpine Club meeting in Denver, Royal told me that he had read this article and liked it.

Robbins - On The Plank

Two of us stroll up the talus toward the base of an obscure vertical wall; my partner, that brown red-breasted bird of the thrush family—with his stares of coldness to conceal warmth. There is a great discharge of silence which follows a cry from my confused stomach. He is noticing everything, the talus stones and ferns, the Longs Peak tundra, Columbines, delicate floral ornamentations, high grasses, and lichen gardens, finding life in even the pores of the granite. Snowfields and nearby Chasm Lake are blinding.

I lead upward on grey rock, ascend with small maraca equipment sounds and tambourine jingles, a gleam of suggestion reflecting out of Royal's strapped-on glasses, me checking my grammar, feeling propelled upward in part by his provoking aura below, sun spilling over him like white water. If he hadn't been a climber he might have lived instead as a mutate from the atomic future, an evil-bearded Cortez of outer solar travel. He stands, a foot forward, his upper half almost leaning backward in defiance, like a fencer. He carries enough passion to subtly electrocute a boulder.

Solid stone, warmth of day, light angling inward from an unobstructed sun, wind blowing, everything steep, curious as it is disorienting. I lead, hanging from pitons which I hope will hold in peculiar cracks which widen inside. Soon I'm on a mossy stance about 100ft. up.

Brown long-sleeve shirt, short-rimmed hat, dark knickers, red knee-socks, boots called Spiders, a carefully combed madness and costume but gentle frowzy sneer, Royal wings up the pitch like a featherweight and with little conversation ascends 90ft. directly overhead, dangling from wizard blades, tiny hooks, rurps, and Chouinard-forged canary toys which support body weight, nothing less, nothing more, because they merely sit, half placed where they should be wholly wedged, balancing where they should be resting. The leader's rope stretches outward through a network of carabiners, whereas the haul line hangs freely away from the wall to indicate perpendicular. In Royal a dangerous eye traverse is followed by an actual ascent exactly that direction, using small nested pitons tied off at the tips. The friend up there is following an innate integrity which translates into purity of line, leading us where nothing looks to be there to climb. Between us is a science-like stream of mechanical coordinations, with the rope as a medium.

To my astonishment — that quality of amazement which makes the mind gaze — Royal yawns, telling me he's off belay. He is going to hang there from a couple of those things and going to bring me up and see if all will hold so that I can collect and bring him some gear, and then I will belay from there as he leads on. There is too much of life in such a setting for it not to be a story to tell. Here, where all of matter seems to be living, then even the smallest flake has a voice.

I hover in comradeship with a mythical Yosemite climber who is meeting me in his journey through Colorado and who climbs now under the guise of acclimatization for a Diamond ascent tomorrow with Layton Kor. It is an experience to be with this unyielding, competitive form — a man so largely self-created. His is an undeniable flair — and the legends are not the man, only the roaring edges of his sea, while somewhere farther out, far away, there is a great calm. The calm is shattered by a carabiner, by the profundity of a beautiful, muted clip. For a few minutes we are personalities without noise, far above a mysterious talus oblivion. A small stone falls, taking seconds to disclose the distance. Royal is drifting, looking downward, possibly thinking of his wife Liz.

As I follow the pitch and Royal belays, he pulls from his shirt pocket a tiny notepad and pen and calmly records information about the pitch, length of lead, number of pitons, weather, partner. What has he said of me? Royal is then snapping photos, one of me framed between his legs. He is a ghostly corona, hanging still like a chairman with a gavel in a cool phantasm. I arrive at the nebulous situation, a right Spider at my head, Royal's toe against the wall, heel in a sling. Here an unbelievable piton has its eye jammed, blade down and not touching rock. I pull up on this piton with all my weight, then notice I can lift it out with a finger. Robbins, face sunburnt. He is covered by a dry perfumed dust like frankincense. He is like a nervous chess piece exposed in the center of the board, castles away into a small corner above — leaving the rook in the open place.

Unexpectedly, as he glances down, our eyes meet, two explosions behind blank despondency. These are rurps, one above the other, us courting a steep, flat surface below a roof and denying rescue of ourselves by rappel. All of it is aid. We would free climb if there were holds. Eventually Royal is going free up a finger crack, building up some noticeable space between him and his last aid point - a hook that swings where it hangs. Nothing between the hook and me looks as though it should stop a fall. Much higher he finds a foothold for belaying and anchors to a solid crack.

I follow the pitch. I rest with my chin for a second on the crook of the hook. I am staring into the filaments of whiskers. Royal, with eminent low voice, says only "Slack," or "OK," if not a witticism barely audible or a pun. With that almost snarl for a smile, he compliments me, saying, "Good boy," which pricks up my ears.

I climb the finger crack above and try to be smooth, measuring myself alongside Robbins. I am impetuous to make a comparison, but that's how I am at about sixteen years old and Royal on toward thirty. Royal, so irreverently disagreeable, but there are methods to his manners. In truth he is a bit shy, neither humble nor self-adoring. Philosophical, brilliant, defensive, cut-throat, he is one of the unique ones. I am asked to go on an errand to find the top. Royal, throwing a gear sling onto my shoulder and me feeling the knighthood, I am leading. I must work for what I achieve, Royal inspiring with a clannish omniscience. Soon the top is obtainable by a short interweaving, a free wall causing at one move a near cramp in a leg for us both.

We stand still, breathing hard and thinking momentarily about his climb, a place we went together out by an edge of an obscure, darkening buttress. The summit is a slope of huge boulders. It is our first climb together, a new route. The Gang Plank, Royal calls it, for it hangs off the side of the Ship's Prow formation. We coil ropes and stumble down the long, tapering, deck side of the rock toward Chasm Lake and then beyond to a rock cabin for shelter. The Diamond Wall, so much larger than what we have done, looms darkly far above. A marmot sniffs Royal from a distance. They turn up their noses at one another...and both are happy.

Royal Robbins on "The Gang Plank" 1964
Photo by Pat Ament

Robbins - On The Plank

In about 1972 I found a publisher for a small book I called "Swaramandal," named after a rare, ancient, eastern Indian musical instrument of ethereal beauty which in the hands of a master would reveal the "sound beyond hearing." I wanted the title to be an illusion to the beauty and hidden meaning that might be found in climbing. A few people thought that it was a bit presumptuous to write an "autobiography" in my early twenties. But nowhere in the book was it advertised as an autobiography. It was rather a "personal mosaic" — a few experiences wherein I was "striving to perceive a pattern." The book concerned itself with friends — climbers such as Kor, Rearick, Gill, Pratt, Robbins, Higgins, and one tiny fourteen-year-old asthmatic with whom I was taken, a boy "as unpretentious as the washed-out photo of him framed to cut off his right ear" (as Tom Higgins later wrote in a review).

Ken Wilson, editor of Mountain Magazine, flattered the book in a review. Higgins, in the American Alpine Journal, gave it another favorable review. He wrote, "Poetic fragments stir our senses and leave us with traces of meaning," and, "Pictures catch personalities off-hand, scrapbook fashion, yielding brief impressions. Here we find the essence of climbing is in fleeting joy and glory, fast moving like cloud shadows on granite, or youthful days in the mountains, forever unretrievable."

As quickly as those golden '60s passed, Swaramandal was out of print and lost to obscurity. Yet a few of its chapters — "Pratt" and "Nerve Wrack Point" — were selected for the anthologies of good climbing writings: The Games Climbers Play, edited by Ken Wilson in 1978, and Mirrors in the Cliffs, edited by Jim Perrin in 1983. "Nerve Wrack Point" was also published in Mountain Magazine in July, 1974.

The following three pieces are from Swaramandal:

Why Roger's Parents Were Worried

The Black Canyon of the Gunnison is narrow, almost hidden. The canyon is situated north of the San Juan mountains, a seven hour drive from Boulder into southwestern Colorado.

The sounds of white water reach the rim of the canyon where Roger Briggs and I stand...staring down. We contemplate dropping a rock and watching it fall. We turn away and walk through a land of trees, sagebrush, and desert silence and descend a gully between the walls.

Ute Indians have a superstitious dread of the Black Canyon and fear evil spirits that dwell in its depths. Winds run through the bends in the canyon like living things.

At the bottom, two thousand foot walls loom above us. The waters of the Gunnison flow westward.

It is autumn and evening. Before sacking out, my fifteen year old comrade and I are challenged by slick, water-polished boulders that submerge in spring. Astral light flashes on the rocks, reflecting a fifty foot flame fueled by piles of driftwood. A night in the deeps.

Huge, jagged, white-pink, pegmatite bands that cross the walls are visible, lit by rays of sunset that bleed into the narrow opening overhead. A night of sounds and imaginings. "Be weird if the water rose tonight," I say to Roger.

Roger and I begin nailing a thin, unflawed, six hundred foot crack at dawn, hacking our way upward into the expanse of the walls.

A traverse eighty feet left where the crack ends takes us across the top edge of a recess which plunges toward our campsite. An elegant, two hundred-foot corner rises from a ledge we are on. I climb up fifty feet in the twilight but return. We bivouac on the ledge.

A light supper...cheese, meat, and water. The sounds of the river below.

Morning. The exposure returns. Scattered clouds and colder temperatures. The top of the corner. Intuition and five hundred feet. A collage of cracks, blocks, and pillars. My friend is subdued, has a far-away look, wonders if I know what I am doing. I wonder too. The ranger is on the rim and shouts down to us.

"Will you make it today?"

"Yes!" I holler back. Roger seems to cheer up.

We reach the summit in dark, stumbling, crawling up a brushy trough like a grave.

Our ride from Boulder to the Black Canyon a one-way affair, we have to figure a way back. The ranger drives us to Montrose, his headquarters seventeen miles southwest. We sleep in the city park, the next morning (trying to hitchhike) suffer police interrogation and have to walk to the ranger's office to borrow bus fare to Grand Junction- the nearest town north. Out of food, hungry, we steal an apple as we pass a fruit stand and snitch candy bars at the bus station. The station master is a chubby Ben Franklin fascinated with us and takes inventory over the top of his bifocals as we leave. The bus is full of Navajo Indians who sing the duration of the ride in the dusk.

Grand Junction's freight yards. The track. The night and wind. A switchman opens a caboose for us. "Warm up. Go to sleep if you want. They'll wake you later," he says.

The caboose has an other-worldly air about it. Briggs resembles a corpse as he dozes. He has a pale complexion. He is really not the silent, stoic type. He is usually light-hearted. But he is worried about his parents, how they will react. He will miss a day of school. He has never ridden the freights. His face is expressionless except for a particular, boyish smile now and then as I boggle his mind with stories of breaking my wrist, a snowstorm on The Yellow Spur, swinging off of Supremacy, and Layton....

Finally I shut up. Roger is tall and thin, with a long, gazelle neck and funny glasses. He is studious, a dean's son, places pitons the way I do....A switch engine slams us. We run out, a train humming, and jump on as it goes. Steel and motion.

We wake up in blackness, suffocating in diesel smoke in the Moffat Tunnel, passing under the Continental Divide, close to home. We wonder if it is night or day. The train's horns blast. We hit East Portal and meet morning, blue skies, and mountain valleys where a foot of snow has fallen.

Pratt

Tom Higgins and I are at the base of El Cap, set on doing a 400ft exfoliation crack called The Slack, a Chuck Pratt masterpiece. This will be a vendetta climb, since we have failed at it before.

After two rope lengths, the flaring section of the crack is in sight. Memories of previous vain motions flash back at us.

It can't be that hard. Pratt did it years ago...on first try. Bridwell hauling me up it my first attempt at it.

I lead. Pratt. Plastic man...or Poe. I grunt and gasp, swing into a layback...I mantel on a ledge above the crux. Higgins follows. Following this one is just as hard. Having the rope in front of you is tricky. You can grab it. Sometimes coming second is harder than leading. You don't have the adrenalin. You have to match the leader's show, but Tom makes it, and we shake hands, grinning at each other.

"I'm tired of being social director of Camp 4," I hear Pratt say to someone pestering him for information. I see Pratt juggling wine bottles at Church Bowl, the clearing east of the lodge. Royal tells tales of Pratt's bouldering drunk, in the dark, in army boots, nobody able to come close. Descriptions of Pratt: a "tragic figure..." or "...born in the wrong time...," yet no climber is more respected or liked in Yosemite. He is hard to figure out and doesn't want to be figured out. "Actions speak for themselves," he says. We hike in the night in the Valley floor. On climbs such as The Slack, one is able to sense the workings of Pratt's mind.

Divergence of contemporary judgments on him. With those he loves, who see him in repose, he is gentle, affectionate, and obliging. He is devoted. Others, who happen to meet him when he is excited, find him irritable, arrogant, self centered, somber, rebellious and go as far as to accuse him of lack of principle or conscience.

Chuck Pratt in the '60s in Yosemite. Photo by Tom Frost

His sensitivity to the beauty and purity to be found in nature, his writing, an account of the South Face of Mount Watkins...The View From Deadhorse Point.... At times, one gets the feeling that Pratt's imagination has taken him away from this earth and the material world into a lonely, personal flight to meditate on ultimate cause and a last climb.

His silence, for some, throws a sullen cloud over his disposition. But he is truly modest, a cat inclined to fits of laughter, to party, or to vanish for weeks. A weird and wily storyteller.... "Nothing worse than a hungry bear," he says. He walks wires. He has nightmares. A soul afflicted with a susceptibility to the effects of beer. The attraction toward it, he does not resist. I have memories of delirious shouts in the Yosemite dark, shouts coming from a short, bald-headed man with a beard.

Fighting to keep his genius clear, to reveal the elements that give the true depth and intensity to the total sheen or dismal glow....

He is a soul with feverish dreams to which he applies a faculty of shaping plausible fabrics out of impalpable materials, with objectivity and spontaneity. He takes, in my mind, a prominent place among universally great men.

Our first big climb together: the North Wall of Sentinel Rock, Pratt's eleventh time up the 1,600ft. face, my second. As he begins the overhang, the fourth pitch of the route, I hear him say softly to himself, "Grown men." We finish the sixteenth pitch in a light, blessing rain.

Nerve Wrack Point

Written with Tom Higgins

Higgins: Life-giving sunlight, positive and harsh on the polished rock, soft and trembling in the grasses. The streams, in their persistent way, oblivious to us, finding the sea. Tuolumne, place of lush, blooming swaths of meadow, of granite domes surrounded by alpine peaks. Summer after summer a handful of climbers come here for the exhilaration of moving on high-angle faces, of teetering a little breathless and spellbound near a sky so blue it seems almost black.

After a short hike, Pat and I are able to get a close look at the southern margin of Lamb Dome, a crackless 500ft. wall. We scramble onto a ledge at the base of the wall.

Climbing this season in Tuolumne has new meaning for me. As I discover more and more my friends, this place, and myself, challenge and difficulty become less insistent, fellowship and encounter more important. I have thoughts of the descent: returning together from the summit, holding and knowing a chosen experience, a chosen day.

It is good to be with Pat. The morning is exquisite. We sort gear and lace our shoes. Feelings are right. We are eager and yet relaxed. Each of us knows the other to be a capable climber. Perhaps I sense a bit of uncertainty in Pat. He is wondering if this will be a competitive ascent.

We rope up.

Pat chalks his fingers. I burrow into some boulders near a tree and secure the belay.

After 40ft. of thin, 70 degree face climbing, he moves left 10ft. to what looks like a crack but isn't. He is able to get a bolt in with half-an-hour of touchy hammering while stemming between two jaw-breaker-sized knobs. Twenty-five feet higher, a second bolt goes. He places the third bolt on a headwall. More thin climbing runs the rope out and takes him to a minimal belay stance. We are happy and loud and imitate the antics of TM Herbert, that light soul, able to laugh and make you feel silly, as opposed to the sometimes snarling ways of climbers.

I follow the pitch. At the belay stance, we begin to realize the seriousness of our undertaking and talk of possible ways to go. The angle of the face appears slightly less to the right. It is 40ft. to the first decent knob. A bolt... maybe... will go there. I work my way up, avoiding anything too hard to reverse. A new route will be a clear-cut achievement for me after months with VISTA where any accomplishment can be easily undone.

I find another crack that isn't a crack, pound the tip of a piton into it, nest another pin behind that one, and tie them off. Contortions. Ament slides his hat off and pushes his fingers through his hair which is a pile of spaghetti stranger than Manzanita. Face climbing without cracks is like roulette. What next?

"We should name this Nerve Wrack Point," Pat suggests. Lamb Dome. Some name for a dome. Lambaste... Lambent... lament...lame...lame-brain.

Ament: I wonder if we will get off in a day. Setting speed records. It's like making love and trying to see how fast you can do it. Higgins is on a nubbin and pressed against the rock...like a butterfly. I study his techniques and strategies, hoping to remember them.

Higgins: Pat blasts loose with a war hoop that sounds like the San Andreas fault shifting. We try to make the difficulties disappear, but they won't. "Exfoliating," I screech.

Ament and his travelling medicine show. Riding freights and cutting records. Walking a tightwire over some canyon in Colorado. Having three affairs all at once.

Ament: Higgins is balancing on an edge. I ask him how it looks.

"Think I see a place where I might be able to get a bolt in."

"Wish Peggy had come climbing with us."

"Look at that blue hat. He sleeps in that thing."

Higgins has a way of getting people outside of themselves. I find myself looking at me.

"It's stupid to push it much further without some protection," Tom says.

"The point of climbing isn't to try to get killed."

Tom's footwork is wild. He gets the bolt in, standing on nothing. An endurance test follows: a 5.9 traverse to the right; two more bolts, the remainder of our supply, widely-spaced.

Higgins: Pat is unpretentious and serious in his appraisal of the situation. While I am climbing, he feeds rope carefully. When I look down I see his body erect, set for a fall, the smiling put aside.

Ament: Tom moves back down to the second from last bolt to set up the belay. This way, the tie-in becomes both the top bolt and the second from last. He belays from two knobs.

I bend and stretch the stiffness out of my muscles. The pitch has taken several hours. I am anxious to move. Finally I am scratching at the rock, straining my eyes in search of crystals. As I arrive at his first bolt, I try to find the footholds he used to place it. I shudder, imagining I'm in the lead. Starting the hard traverse, I stop and stare at it. My rope leads to the side here. I am not in love with the idea of swinging fifty feet and inch out onto the traverse, reciting the lyrics of a tune by The Grateful Dead.

"Three feet and you'll be able to see a pebble for your right foot," Higgins maintains. I spread-eagle to it. When I arrive up he hurries me by, clipping onto me the few chunks of hardware we have brought. I picture him speeding along in his Porsche...(he drives a Volks, is obsessed with Porsches).

Higgins: Ament says something to the rock from behind the chalk trapped between his lips. But nothing happens except he drops the chalk. I'm making little curse noises from my belay, thinking we might not make it, and humming. I hum to the rock. A crazy combo of some blues piece and Erik Satie coming out in little push-breaths.

Ament is both afraid and fearless, working upward on hard moves, complaining that his sunburn is bad and that he expects to faint soon.

Ament: The rock is steeper. I talk to the butterflies in my stomach. Old aspirations. No possible protection. Higgins flicks the rope. It jerks me, almost pulls me off. Tom leans his head against the rock, baking in the sun. I pick out holds.

"Taking plenty of time and making sure I don't fall."

"Don't blame you. Take all the time you want."

"If I can just reach that thing up there..."

"Looks like a good hold."

"I guess I sort of have to commit myself."

"Go for it."

"I couldn't climb down that last stretch anyway, so..."

"I'm watching you."

"There. Got it."

"The rope's stuck down here. Climb back so I can free it."

"Huh?!"

"Just kidding."

Disappearing over the top of a bulge, I find a ledge which is a relief. Maybe the ledge is a mirage. I bring Higgins up. Our feet are dead from edging. My sunburn is beginning to take the joy out of the climbing. We have reached a point high enough to see over a hill to a glimmering edge of Tenaya Lake. A breeze blows across the wall. I have thoughts, I am young and it is winter, reverberations of river and pine... in Eldorado Canyon... and Kor. In memory, Eldorado takes on the essence of a supernatural canyon. It is as if I can feel, as if I have felt before, the afternoon flight of the shadows up the walls; the higher summits still lit; birds coasting beside the buttresses and landing on ledges. I imagine myself at the end of a tightwire, looking across it, the ghost of Ivy Baldwin with me. A cable strung over a canyon, challenging me.

"Higgings   Skwigglins."

"You're flipping, Ament. It was all of those avocados you ate on the drive up."

"Tom Horrendo and Pat Amazing."

"Look at him. Gone."

Tom is leading above me on a vertical corner that arches to the summit. The bottoms of his shoes show. If he comes off, I'll go home with footprints on my face. Now what's he doing? With his foot over his ear...

Higgins: The last lead is short. Still hard, though. The most direct way simply will not go. I am forced right, onto a long sliver of a ledge that feels rotten. What if the ledge stayed but the wall fell off...? Friction above the ledge, then the summit of Lamb Dome. Sitting down to unlace my shoes, they are already unlaced. Imagine that. As I pull in the rope, Pat holds more chalk between his lips. We are still playing the game, making much of a short and terribly improbable climb. When the climb is finished, we take one another's picture. The camera fixes our images like those of miners I recall seeing in brown and faded photos, arms slung around the nearest co-worker, companions just up from another day of beating stone, cursing money and fate. Pictures remind me of miners, grandfathers, and death. Pat is caught awkward and smiling. I am relaxed and dazed. In the future I will feel a loss when coming across these photos. Looking down, the sheets and sheets of it seem as though they should be an endless aid-job. Except the beauty has gone free. We turn toward the east. Long, dome shadows are on the meadows. We were permitted to pass.

Ament descends the easy slopes of granite before me, camera jostling at his side. I try not to like him too much, but... it is no less than love I feel for Pat, myself, and this day. Much says no to the sense of intimacy: my headlong pursuit of far off personal goals, the shambles of several marriages among friends. Who is Ament? I think. Who is Higgins? Pat thinks. We are two souls moving together from the summit of a dome, wars waging themselves to the east, traffic toiling below, a brief ascent securing within us unexplainable but real joy.

Ament: I am standing in San Francisco International Airport. It is nine o'clock at night. I am gazing at a runway through my reflection in a window. I will have to wait here all night, a new kind of bivouac, having missed my plane. I am duped by a suspicious desk clerk, Susie United, who senses that my youth card is phony.

"What's your date of birth?" she asks.

"1951," I reply.

"How old are you?"

"Uhhh...sixteen."

"I'll have to talk to my supervisor about this!"

I'm blushing, be-fuddled, with swirls of blonde hair, black and sleezy trench coat, a bomb in my suitcase.

Put Higgins in this situation. I see him gracing through it... with his fancy footwork, his full, barrel-chested laugh. I don't mesh with the gears of society. Quite the contrast: San Francisco International Airport and Tuolumne — our pastoral land of Oz.

I miss the last plane while waiting for the additional money to be sent. A night stranded here! Some joke. My parents are waiting to pick me up at the airport in Denver. They'll appreciate it when I don't show. Can't call Peggy. She's deserted me, gone east for awhile. Nerve Wrack Point, the climbing, our friendship.... The mountains teach us of the joys that are ours. I will be like Hig: buoyant, never morose.

Voices. Paging me? "Paging Pat Ament, paging Pat Ament, your Rolls Royce is waiting for you out in front...."

Maybe I'll call Higgins and listen to him laugh. Miss him already. Kind of hate going back to Colorado, in some ways. Higgins' routes. He believes in the improbable, "thy will be done." Our respective climbing teachers are themselves best friends: Rearick and Bob Kamps. We are indeed friends. Though somehow ... alone. Me searching for companionship, living for the day. Higgins, VISTA volunteer, with a future, keeping cool. He'll grow old. One fault of Higgins', he's persnikety. He's never yet lived in Camp 4 because he'd have to share his utensils!

You get the feeling that climbing stories are written in dark, music filled studies, or on the summits themselves. Words chiseled into granite...in Greek. So maybe San Francisco International will be some kind of first. Airports seem geared for 1990. People, all different weird kinds, movie stars, lawyers, Cubans, with tickets to Australia and New Jersey. Soldiers. The roar of planes taking off....

Dawn...it is time to go, at last. Got the ticket, received my money. I'll see you, Tuolumne, next summer. Higgins, I'll see you.

Upon the unfortunate death of climber-publisher Bob Godfrey in spring of 1988, a death by suicide, I was allowed a few of his books. In one I noticed some words Bob had underlined: "Men kill themselves because they are afraid of death," a line by Robert Creeley.

I worked with Bob on any number of projects, the first of which was his book "Climb," published in 1977 wherein I recall the events of the first ascent of Supremacy Crack, a climb of the mid-'60s that gained notoriety.

A Brief Supremacy

Supremacy Crack has a history which may be amusing and perhaps slightly gratifying to climbers who are intrigued by the origins and lore of such extremes. The discovery of Supremacy Crack must be credited to Dave Rearick. A morning in 1965, he showed me the diabolical, twenty-foot slit.

We drove up the canyon, past the main climbing area of Eldorado, to the provocative, hidden crack piercing the south side of a quartzite slab. Dave had a grin on his face instead of the usual austere look. In his mind he was seeing me swing off the crack on his old, white, hopelessly frayed Diamond rope, about which he was sentimental. Dave scrambled the easy way to the top, doubled the rope down from a piton anchor, returned, and had me tie-in. He sat down with the rope around him, half knowing the route would go. A fall meant a sixty-foot swing above the river, and the bottoms dropped out of our stomachs when we thought about it. Instructed to practice the swing in order to get rid of the fear of it, I made a move upward, reluctantly, glanced with wide eyes at Rearick's happy face, was overcome with a weak, hysterical sensation, and let go. I was like a ball of gum spinning slowly away from him on a strand of hair. When it was his turn, Dave much preferred climbing up and jumping off to giving the crack a serious attempt. Every kid sooner or later finds a rope to swing on — Tarzan style — across a river. Rearick was in his thirties.

For the most part, Supremacy Crack was a place to play. We never thought of leading it or doing it "in style." We scarcely gave it a "best effort" and did not consider it a failure because we were able to do a third of it. There was no reason to believe that it would ever be respected by climbers. Part of the reason I brought other climbers to look at Supremacy and try it with me was that it was fun. It was a conversation-piece, something to wonder about. Bob Culp held the rope, yawned and chuckled as I played. Tex Bossier tried to motivate me with ravings that what was happening was incredible.

I was never really good enough to do the climb until my mental attitude toward it changed. Instead of viewing it as fun, it became a fevered, exotic dream, a priority for me with a certain oozing charm, and with Roger Rauback belaying I found myself mesmerized to the rock, struggling, applying a certain integration of mind and touch, and succeeding. Roger's face seemed to get red and puffy as he exclaimed, somewhat belatedly, "You did it!"

The crack immediately developed a reputation in Colorado and in other areas of the United States. While actually surprised by this, I was at the same time proud to have made the first ascent.

About a year later, after climbing Ruper in Eldorado, I brought my two companions to Supremacy. It was a hot afternoon, and a lot of people with equipment were wandering around the canyon. My companions were both better climbers than I, and it was my feeling that one of them might enjoy doing the first leading ascent of Supremacy. They were Royal Robbins and Don Whillans.

I expected a day of humility and was sure that the myth of Supremacy would be dissolved. Whillans hinted that routes like Supremacy were a six pence a dozen in England. Earlier in the day, on Ruper, he had led both the crux pitches entirely unprotected and exhibited amazing form. On the Ruper crack, the rope from Whillans ran down freely to me and was between Royal and the rock. Royal stood unanchored, and I whispered nervously to him, "If Whillans falls, he'll yank you off." "I'll take that chance," Royal replied.

After the three of us arrived at Supremacy, there appeared a group of tourists and climber spectators ready to witness the absurdity. Royal went a few moves up the crack and placed a nut. It was my first introduction to the use of nuts for protection. He then rather quickly decided that I should lead, since I was familiar with the climb. It was hard to know what to make of Royal's machine nuts with slings through them, apparently the newest of his creative whims. The easiest and most efficient method of protecting such a lead was at hand, but I didn't know it. I grabbed some pitons, a few carabiners, and a hammer.

First to belay me, Whillans provided added incentive by keeping a lot of slack in the rope and staring soberly into space. I jammed up the first crux, hung there with one hand half-wedged, placed a piton, clipped the rope through, and lowered to the belay. Whillans gave Royal the rope and went off to spread out a blanket by the river and lie in the sun. I led past the second crux, hung again by a poor hand jam, placed a second piton, clipped in, and again returned for a breather. After shaking out my arms, I climbed to the high point, proceeded higher, got a third piton in somewhere near the top, moved back to the second piton, rested briefly there with the help from the piton, then went up the remainder of the way to the top. Having upper-belayed the climb the previous year proved of little help, since the sequence used now was completely different than any before. It was obviously not a climb one could readily "wire." Hardly a perfect lead, but a few satisfying moments were spent alone at the summit before scrambling down the back way to belay Royal. It was quite a view from the summit with high country sparkling to the west, with the warm yellow Eldorado walls rising to the east, with green trees and blue sky everywhere and Whillans below showing no signs of movement, undoubtedly drifting into a sleep.

Royal followed the crack, only using aid through one section. His showing was better than my first top-rope try. I had always liked Royal's technique and been able to learn something from observing it. Here was no exception.

When Whillans was ready to leave America and return to England, he stopped at my house. We traded a few final laughs and reflections about climbing. He speculated that I would never really get much better than I was the day on Supremacy. He was speaking of spiritual things before I was old enough to understand them. I gave him some American currency in exchange for a lot of foreign coins which had been a nuisance to him, and he thanked me with a photo he'd taken of Supremacy. I've kept those coins, that lousy far-off photo, and whenever I stumble across them I experience a full range of emotion, remembering the stimulus, the dizzy unveiling of possibilities, of the '60s.

Pat Ament 'with' Bob Dylan

The following chapter is selected from Master Of Rock because of the several favorite bouldering areas it recalls for me, places which—when revisited—continue to inspire and bring memories of my incredible friend John Gill.

In 1977 I wrote "Master of Rock," an appreciation of John Gill. The word "biography" was added at the publisher's request, although I did not feel that the writing was extensive enough to be called so. It was a book about climbing, and climbing was only one manifestation, one metaphor, of Gill's spirit. I wrote the book without telling Gill and presented it to him after it was completed. One section of the book was a "fireside chat" I obtained under the auspices of narration for a possible film. Gill was surprised but also tolerant when I showed him what I created. Undoubtedly I injected too much of myself into the book, but I felt it important to convey what Gill and I had shared bouldering together.

Gill was, in the late '50s and early '60s, the true pioneer of extreme gymnastic climbing and, all things considered, is unsurpassed even as of 1990. He set a standard so far ahead of its time that climbers tended to dismiss him. His bouldering accomplishments represented a threat to the comparatively mediocre standards of others. Even the strongest rock climbers today owe much of what they have achieved to the consciousness brought to climbing by Gill.

When Bob Godfrey got wind of the book, he asked to publish it. We were supported in its printing by the legendary publisher Fred Praeger, although the first printing was, foolishly, a run of only two thousand. It sold out quickly. As always, I became absorbed in other creative delusions and had no time to go back to old projects. Although in 1984 the book was published in Japan—the text done in lovely Japanese characters. The much needed example of John Gill, his humility, intelligence, spiritual strength, and ability, have transcended the age in which he passed through bouldering areas almost as a myth. In 1986 and 1987, he was honored by the American Alpine and British Mountaineering Clubs. I was fortunate to be able to go with him to England.

A Profiled Position

Six-foot-two, a hundred and eighty pounds, and able to do a one-arm, one-finger pullup, Gill is attracted to the more immediately gratifying or perhaps frustrating type of climbing which requires the use of such strength. West of Fort Collins, Colorado, are short sandstone cliffs covered with routes done by him. In 1968 Gill and I were climbing in this area.

I watched him flow up horrendous overhangs with exasperating ease, the area illuminated by the finesse he employed. My excruciating forays were comical, yet Gill was patient and helpful. As I was beginning a route of his, I was able to recall a letter I received in 1966. Royal Robbins had written the encouraging words, "Sounds as if your strength and gymnastic ability are formidable. You should soon step into Gill's shoes as the boulder king of the U.S." I was in an awkward position and lunged for what I thought was a hold. In the twinkling of an eye, I returned—with amazing speed—to where I had started. I sat upon the ground with unspeakable pain penetrating my tailbone. Step into Gill's shoes? For the remainder of the day I enjoyed the role of observer.

Through the beauty of his creations, the mentality of the man was expressed. There was substance to Gill's climbing and to his quiet manner. With a refined outlook and carefully tempered hunger for perfection, he traversed, superbly balanced, into a profiled position. It was a blending of insight, muscle, and technique. A climbing world needed a John Gill to humble it... and to inspire it.

In 1968 at Split Rocks, an area located approximately halfway between Boulder and Estes Park, Colorado, Gill and I climbed the better part of a day. Jagged granite blocks strewn throughout the forest tore the flesh of fingertips and shredded egos. A warm sun made the day pleasant, and we discovered every technique, every sort of problem. I was a little afraid to try a few of the routes which Gill ascended with authority.

When he spoke, it was as though his voice was in some deep cavity resonating. Low and commanding, it was rarely heard except for a "ho ho" in response to my struggles.

He approached a smooth, overhanging, fifteen-foot wall and, at first, gently drew breath. Then his eyes became fixed on a high hold. While compressing his upper torso, as if to recoil, he began to hyperventilate loudly. To follow was a perfectly calculated, slow-motion leap. There was a subtle, although important, shuffling of his feet on tiny nubbins. One hand reached over the rounded summit, the other pulled laterally. It was quick, and he hurled himself to the top of the boulder.

I squeezed the initial holds and sighed. I could grasp the holds but not the problem. After examining the fifteen-foot wall closely, it was, to me, the beauty and savoir-faire of Gill.

To be a disciple of his would be, I felt, an honor. I followed him about the boulders religiously, hoping for him to bestow in me some hidden knowledge of the art. He tried to dispel my romantic notions with realistic talk, insisting that he had lots of weaknesses and that I was the real climber because I did longer routes and big-wall ascents.

We rigged a top rope, and Gill belayed me on a delicate wall. Initially I was uncertain as to how to start. The only foothold was roughly the size of a pencil eraser. If I dislocated my shoulders I could reach, for the left hand, a slippery pinch-edge and, for the right, a sickeningly small, sharp, fingertip flake. There was little advantage in knowing that John had climbed the route and judged it to be moderate! In his presence, I found that I could push myself farther than I'd planned. I got a hand on the bucket-hold at the top before my weight went onto the rope. On a later visit to Split Rocks, I made the delicate wall and repeated it a number of times because it seemed to bring Gill to me when he was not there.

Upon discovering one of his tiny chalk arrows drawn on the rock near the bottom of certain deserving problems, a climber is able to intuit Gill's capacity for choosing an aesthetic line. These routes are delicate, accurate, full of interesting nuances of character.

I stood underneath one such route at Castle Rock, west of Boulder, Colorado, in 1969. Two small holds arrested the eye but were the only flaws in rounded, overhanging, bulging granite which arched out above a tiny, white arrow. I could tell that I would have to search deep in order to see the solution to the moves. I wanted to see with Gill's eye. I approached the holds but was unable to find a sequence which worked. I resorted to my right heel hooked on a tiny edge above my head, my hands crossed on a finger-tip crack, and left foot frictioning on lichen. Talus below made me reluctant to extend myself, yet unlikely contortions and hard pulling brought me to a ledge at the end of the route. By identifying with Gill, I was able to succeed.

In 1969, I was sitting alone in a deserted Camp 4, the bouldering area of Yosemite. Pine needles were in my shoes, and chalk that I had been rubbing on my fingers was in my hair. The boulders had worn me out after a couple of hours of climbing them. A breeze blew through the lofty trees, and I gazed upward at surrounding walls of granite which rose thousands of feet. A waterfall roared in the distance. The Sierra scene, spring smells, sun, and the sky were telling me to look beyond the surface of climbing.

I was homesick for Colorado, yet persuaded to remain in Yosemite by some spell.

I began to reflect upon bouldering, its loneliness and frustration. In the hot afternoon, a drop of sweat in my palm became a crystalline image. John Gill was encouraging me to laugh at myself, because I was too serious. In the little drop, I saw Gill caress the underside of an overhang, cling to it, then launch himself like an arrow upward toward some doubtful set of holds. I felt the intrigue of a man whose name was blowing softly through the forests of the Grand Tetons, the South Dakota Needles, Colorado, and many areas. I had visited Yosemite a number of times with increasing success on the boulders and realized that my new exertions were due, in part, to Gill. I felt that what I was doing on the boulders of Camp 4 was leaving a small mark, a few first ascents of my own which would perhaps speak of what I had learned from someone whose skill was superior.

I wanted to be one with the rock instead of at war with it. It was an odyssey of mood filling me with a desire to climb hard but with a meticulous feel. I was charged with the electricity of Gill's touch, with the reinforcement of his character transmitting to me from a distance. I was drawn to this contemplation but also satisfied with just lazily sitting, intoxicated with bouldering. In a momentary nostalgic feeling, a drop of sweat dissolved into callous.

After returning to Colorado I bouldered several times with Gill. On Flagstaff Mountain and in Eldorado Canyon, he did many of my best problems. We visited some granite along the Gem Lake

Trail near Estes Park and pushed our limits at Split Rocks. At Fort Collins Gill came out to the cliffs with me but did not attempt to climb, because he had suffered a torn ligament in his elbow. The injury was a nightmare to him. The extent and seriousness of it were unknown, and it was accompanied by extreme pain, prohibiting him from doing even the simplest problems. We hiked to a forest west of Horse Tooth Reservoir, where boulders awaited exploration, and I made the first ascent of a red, bulging wall which Gill gave to me since it would have been his. I was in my best physical and mental shape ever, and Gill, although depressed about his elbow, was inspired. The frustrations of his injury seemed to diminish with just the thought of climbing.

An evening on Flagstaff Mountain, overlooking the city of Boulder, Colorado, I climbed alone and was able to surpass some of my own goals on the coarse sandstone upon which I had worked for many years. I tested myself, moved as gracefully as possible, and felt complete composure. Gill's example was becoming a strong influence in my climbing and was beginning to play a significant role in my development. Flagstaff was full of light and autumn. I thought about Gill's injury and wondered if he was finished.

In the middle of winter, 1975, I bouldered with him in the badlands west of Pueblo, Colorado, and found that he was far from incapacitated. Many climbers had thought he would never again reach his previous standard. Indeed, Gill could not be eclipsed by time or injury. He had recovered and, although acutely aware of the possibility of reinjury, climbed brilliantly. He showed me a route which he had achieved, a ferocious, twenty-foot, overhanging arete called "The Little Overhang." This name was derived because the route was below another larger overhang. It exhilarated me when John gave the much higher overhang an inquisitive stare.

I was amazed that Gill could find a bouldering area near Pueblo. He employed his sixth sense for discovering perfect little outcrops that just suited him. The routes were all very difficult, and I was impressed enough to want to make a 16mm movie, a documentary of his form and style in bouldering. Gill had to be captured on speeding film. The first day of shooting, however, was a disaster. The camera I'd rented didn't work. It would run for about fourteen seconds, then stop. Gill was aware of the camera, especially when, at the crux move, it would click off! It gave us a few laughs, for example when, as he hung in the middle of an overhang, I snorted, "The camera quit, can you hold it there?"

In February, 1976, I visited the Hagermeister boulders, near Estes Park, with a young climber of prodigious talent and originality, David Breashears. A cold wind kept us from climbing, so we toured the rocks. I pointed out Gill routes. I saw in David's eyes an energy. He thought of bouldering someday with Gill. It seemed Gill's inspiration was to touch yet another generation. Just by glancing at gray, lifeless rock, a respect for Gill could generate. I recalled visiting this place before ever meeting John, in days when his strength was spoken of but rarely seen. I had searched out the area after hearing that a superhuman climber from the Needles had done several routes which would never be repeated. Some never have.

John Gill
Photo by Pat Ament

In September of 1964, when I had just turned eighteen, I rode a freight train from Fresno, California, to Denver, Colorado. It was a way to get home from Yosemite after my first trip there with Royal Robbins. I shivered in my sleeping bag on a flat car in a snowstorm, through Eldorado Canyon at sunrise. I remained attracted to the somewhat boyish idealism of freight trains, and when spring would roll around I would roll away on a freight train toward Yosemite. I once used the freights to visit a girlfriend in California. The freights gave a beautiful, reflective view of the mountains, deserts, and rolling prairie of the western United States, but also instilled in me certain feelings I would like to refer to as mystical.

The following article tries to address such feelings and was published in Mountain Magazine, October 1981.

A freight train ascends in a canyon,
through a tunnel, through starlight.
Wind, rock, red. It corners a bank above a river.
Coyote country. Lizard country. Spires.
Shrill screams of wheels,
silence ·in every distance.
I bolt upright out of a dream
into the flickering sky of the Utah desert,
a hobo on a flatcar
like the form of the shroud of Turin,
cinders in my eyes, earth, sage, flower,
the sweet breath of the desert
blowing
in my face
like   resurrection.

Reason Does Not Know

Some of the finer moments of climbing have been spent in freight yards, on freight trains, on the way to or from rock climbing areas.

One of the most formidable mantels I ever performed was onto a moving flatcar with a heavy pack on my back, my feet swinging underneath - almost brushing the wheels. One of the worst falls I took in climbing was off a freight train going forty miles per hour through Sacramento, California, on the way to Yosemite. It was a moment of indecision, as in climbing, when you're not certain whether to hang on or get off. I got off, end-over-end down an embankment.

There are climbers who feel at home in the freight yards, at ease with the grime and the adventure. Young and in the army, Royal Robbins while on a weekend leave rode the freights back to California to climb. An exciting moment saw him leap from the top of one moving boxcar to another.

I was once arrested for riding the freights. The police escorted me to the nearest bus station. After waving farewell to them, I found my way back to the freight yards to resume my trip more inconspicuously.

During the golden age of Yosemite climbing, in the '60s, all a climber needed were a few leftovers, perhaps a sympathetic woman, one shirt, one tattered pair of pants, and a little knowledge of the freight lines. With bare billfolds, a few of us had some of the best summers of our lives. A season in Yosemite was followed by a meditative freight trip home, with the Utah desert a reflection of El Cap — brown, vast, hot, and endless. In Eldorado Canyon, the train passes through several tunnels near some spectacular climbs on a rock called the Mickey Mouse. Climbers must walk through the tunnels as an approach to those routes, an approach where a climber may encounter an oncoming train.

I rode to Yosemite on the freights from Colorado many times, acquiring a black face from the tunnels, nestling softly at night in smoky boxcars or on piggyback carriers, rattling through sage hills, dining in the brush with hoboes. The hobo world is one of character, of integrity, souls like the most brilliant and surly of climbing, hard men. I felt a kindred spirit in the many travellers with whom I conversed, rode, ate, and waited, with whom I shared adverse weather.

I recall Simon, in Salt Lake City. Just out from a month in a California jail "for drinkin," he was on the way to a job he'd heard about: picking peaches in Grand Junction, Colorado. He was cold. I gave him the orange cagoule I wore on El Cap. An orange cagoule looks in most ways out of place on a black hobo, but he wore it proudly. He felt close to that coat and would not remove it even as our train hit the hundred-degree heat of the desert. As on a bivouac, we shared some pittances of food—bread and lettuce.

Through Colorado at night, I rode with a man who looked a bit like Woody Guthrie. "Got a little cold there over the mountains," he commented as we rolled into Denver at dawn. It had been unbearably cold. In a coat and sleeping bag I was hypothermic, while he had no sleeping bag and only a light tweed jacket. He spent that cold night sitting up, smoking cigarettes, thinking, observing the dark.

Jim Allen and I divided my last six dollars in a freight yard in Stockton, California. His small white dog Skinner was in need of a meal. As far as Jim was concerned, Skinner came first. Business had been sparse for this wiry, lean man who collected scrap metal and sold it to a junkyard for fifty-six cents a pound. I thought of the pitons in my pack.

Standing under the stars late at night in a Fresno, California train yard, when I was eighteen, I listened to the stories of Will Noel who stood in a suit and tie, barefoot. His hands had been broken badly by two men who smashed them against the track. They stole his money, his shoes, and his hat. This little black man repeated, "May the Lord strike me with lightning if I'm lyin." I did not doubt him, yet adrenalin placed a few steps between him and me, as if for safety. He shook my hand and said I was the only person who had listened to him ever in his life. To this moment I experience a quiet feeling when I recall Will Noel disappear away slowly by himself into the California dark.

I remember sharing a few thoughts with another lonely hobo in a different California yard. No dusk could eclipse his forsaken, squinting gloom, as he sat clutching a full, unopened bottle of wine, resisting it, hoping to make it go far, perhaps forever, a man enduring, craving a sip, a bottle that was his glimmer of hope, a pale, thorny, rugged, nervous face pink in the twilight, eyes lit with the desire for a train. A soul regretful but unashamed, sitting beside the track, half camouflaged in weeds. I drew briefly upon his wisdom which he shared with glances and select raspy words. He pointed toward a track I needed to watch. As I walked away, a diesel was moving rapidly through the yard, a train with a flatcar carrying two men - one black, one brown. The black man jumped from the car and ran toward my hobo friend who sat hypnotized and off guard. From a distance, I observed the black man grab the precious bottle of wine and continue in stride running back toward the train which increased quickly in speed. The black man ran as fast as legs could sprint in the cinders, trying to catch the train. An outstretched palm received first the bottle, then the black man's hand. Their miracle was made, as he crawled onto the flatcar, and they headed south with a bottle to become then the sordid meaning of their lives. I caught sight of my hobo friend sitting still, slowly shaking his bowed head with a smile, radiating from that distance an unspeakable emptiness, a final peace which I sensed should remain his alone, causing me to turn and continue along my way—once again leaving some part of me behind.

I cannot forget the yardsmen and the engineers who guided me along these years, who woke me out of a sleep to warn me that the car I was on had to be left behind, or who brought me into a caboose to be out of the wind, who filled my waterbottles and traded stories with me. In Salt Lake City, an engineer slowed his train down so that I could get on.

I have an image of an eagle squatting atop a telegraph wire, watching me rattle by, somewhere in the badlands of Nevada. There are memories of counting ties, wire-walking rails, writing songs in my imagination. I recall terror, mental anguish, insecurity, and loneliness produced in me certain nights, occasions when I felt isolated, at the mercy of moving steel, dreams, and darkness. Through mystical canyons, beside rivers, windblown, using cardboard for a blanket, along foothills green with spring, over ridges of flowers, through alfafa, through seasons, through the Moffat Tunnel, the banging choking ink of night. After my first trip to Yosemite, I rode home through Eldorado Canyon at break of day, the climbs of Eldorado as lonesome for me as I for them, their rock towers silhouetted against a sky I had never seen so red.

There is train blood in me. My father worked seventeen years for the Rio Grande in Denver. He knows the feelings. My mother lived aside the tracks as a young girl whose friend was killed by a freight train. She knows the dangers.

I still dream of trains, of loud stormy darkness, of motion. Anymore, when I am making any decision, if I hear the horn of a freight train I consider it more than coincidence—rather a confirmation. Trains symbolize freedom, years of youthful adventure. A lost soul or a poor soul, a victim, a sullen spirit, a drunk, a fugitive, a climber or a drifter, someone too depressed, one too much of a genius to cope with mortality, hard suffering individuals with stares or laughing voices, twisted sunburned faces, hoarse, mumbling, insane shadows, sad hopeless souls, yet something inside them worthwhile, decent, insightful, or pure. The philosopher

Pascal states, "the heart has its reasons which reason does not know."

Freights are like rocks. Both rise ominously above you in the starlight, secret, dangerous, both convey the magical, the mysterious, both vehicles to carry one toward sleep, or awakening, toward life that is alluring, robbing, and elusive like a bottle of wine held by a hobo, life which waits many times somehow in the distance, always a journey, but never far.

Coming home from Yosemite by way of freight train, 1967. Photo by Pat Ament.

My tiny book "Direct Lines" was typed rather than type-set, and distributed very sparsely. I thought that if I could sell a few copies, I might keep from starving another week. I sold every copy quickly, and the book was so well liked by Dr. Jim Perrin, one of England's top climbing writers, that I was invited to be a guest speaker for the National British Mountaineering Conference. Perrin wrote in High Magazine, March 1984, "Direct Lines is one of the two best books of essays in its field by one author to have been published since Patey and Murray."

Bouldering With My Mom

It was Christmas season, 1981. I found myself in San Diego, California, visiting my parents who were there for the winter. Colorado was ice and snow, so it was a pleasure to greet the warmth of Southern California. Roger Barnes, a friend and climber living in San Diego, proposed rock climbing — specifically bouldering on nearby Mt. Woodsen. My parents went along.

My parents have always been somewhat supportive of rock climbing and have watched from a distance as I have taken this bohemian route in my life. My father kept scrambling the easy way to the top of each boulder, claiming to be the better climber. My mother, sunny, happy, huffed and puffed along with us, at one point struggling with a little bout with asthma.

Our group included several school kids and transient juveniles, a few with long hair, looking as though they should have a surfboard under one arm. There was Roger, a sort of paternal friend to them.

Young terrors reeked of expectation, hoping I would perform.

It was a group of climbers in a sort of trendy, immature world of our own. To have parents come into it was strange.

For the most part I was lazy and out of shape. Winter had added fifteen pounds to an ever slowing metabolism. The Californians seemed to remain in form year round. They treated me kindly. It appeared my stature as a climber was enough to have earned a certain lethargy. The classic routes on Mt. Woodsen could be managed without great stress, and experience allowed for quick recognition of a few problematic combinations. Yet I was unwilling to push my limits, for fear of embarrassing myself.

Finally I was enticed into putting a couple of fingers into a beautiful, irresistible, but very difficult crack. The competitive spirit took hold. One or two of the climbers demonstrated the little crack, admitting they had worked on it many weeks before ever luckily solving it. I stood looking at the route, socializing, chalking my hands, wondering how I might grace through. I stood procrastinating, shooting the breeze, commenting on the warmth, on my sweaty fingers, a body leaning against the rock, feeling the first move and re-feeling, discouraged, dull, hindered, a notion of defeat pleasing to my carnal mind, when suddenly, at the most inconvenient moment of weakening resolve, my mother spoke:

"I'm getting tired of waiting, now stop standing there, and get up that rock!"

She startled me, with a typical mother's boldness, with authority and impertinence cutting through the stature, the facades, and the hard-man veneers.

No climber could have applied this much pressure. I found myself moving unhesitatingly upward, calling forth the most straightforward of techniques—graceful or otherwise to the top.

Luisa and Heinz

In 1980 in Yosemite, I met Luisa Iovane and Heinz Mariacher. She was from Venice, Italy, and he from somewhere in Austria. They spoke different dialects of German and Italian but could communicate with one another. They were traveling together apparently as boy and girlfriend. She spoke a small measure of English. I knew three words of German: "Schnell" (quickly) and "von hinden" (from behind) which were chess phrases I had learned from a German chess player.

Luisa and Heinz were exceptional climbers and people. They casually ascended several of the big routes on El Capitan, bringing no bivouac gear (outside of a light parka each), eating very little food, and not bothering with a haul bag. The three of us became friends. There seemed to be a communication apart from words. Occasionally Luisa would understand something I said and would attempt to translate it to Heinz. But the rope was enough of a link between friends. Heinz spoke the universal language of chess in Yosemite Lodge each night, and there was a certain very attractive body language coming from Luisa. Heinz lost every game of chess, and I sensed he became mildly competitive — as though to save face with Luisa. A last straw was that I had to rescue him as he attempted a solo climb one day and became stuck. Luisa belayed me as I led to him.

It was beginning to look like the classic case where two is company, but three...

And I admit it did cross my mind that had I not rescued Heinz, Luisa would have been left to me.

Luisa Iovane

Heinz Mariacher

We played Frisbee in the campground.

Around the fire at night I had Luisa help me compose a love letter in German for a girlfriend in Colorado who was taking a German class. Heinz was quiet. After the letter was done, Luisa said, in so many mixtures of English, Italian, and German that she wished Heinz could write such a beautiful letter to her.

I really did not know what the letter said, but it was becoming clear that Heinz and Luisa had something. I would not let any temporary lust of my own stand in the way. Besides, I had a girl friend in Colorado. Why should I tamper with their little flight together? We shared a number of short but good climbs, then sadly parted ways, three friends communicating respect and trust more effectively than could we had there been words. I tried not to read too much into the fact that my Colorado girlfriend, soon after receiving that letter in German, wrote me a dear John.

Airy Dares

Late summer, 1982, I was searched out by a certain very beautiful pediatrician for climbing lessons. All of a sudden the oldness of instruction seemed reconcilable.

Here was one of those obvious detours in life where the sensual mind rises up in a great flurry, bringing the inner spirit and much more appropriate perspectives into subjection. As I led her up climbs, I found myself conversing in baby talk.

"Has he always been this way?" I heard her ask a mutual climbing friend, as though preparing a diagnosis.

I was oblivious to the strata of the rock, distracted by her sinewy form.

In Eldorado Canyon, a few miles south of Boulder, Colorado, on a chilly early morning prior to climbing, she bet me a hundred dollars I wouldn't jump into the river. The water looked very cold, but an impoverished climber will go to almost any extreme to win a woman's affections and make money doing it. On the other hand, if I doused myself, that would be all the less money she would have for climbing lessons. I stood on the point of a rock, half-undressed, contemplating the pros and cons. I decided not to take the dare, knowing I would get the hundred one way or another.

I tried to trap us hundreds of feet up on climbs in the rain or other storms where she might be forced to cuddle with me at belay ledges, where the hero could deliver her up a wall to safety.

It was high on the Yellow Spur route of Eldorado, as lightning threatened to change me into a pair of climbing shoes and embers, that I examined my motives.

Yet it was the Eldorado emporium in full, vertigos, axis points, to balance at and shiver in, germane, pertinent, a strange ethereal scherzo of inward feelings, the delicious ionosphere of rock climbing, an iridescent interplay of mood and life, contrasts, perplexities, converging, out of darkness, into great light and space, the real double-entendre, two people, two meanings, non-entity, totalness.

"Paying attention?" she asked at a hard section as I stared outward while belaying.

She brought me to an expensive restaurant and wore a loose, white, silky, see-through dress so translucent I found it difficult to swallow.

We bouldered in moonlight, participated in private extravaganza picnics, greasy lips, hand-feeding one another barbequed game hen, discussing religion and divergent life plans.... We picnicked at drive-in movies, picnicked on one another in summer evenings of passion. Our energies were lavish. She rode a bike forty miles to see me, or drove those miles in a rain with broken wipers. I did more climbing than I had in seasons. Hundreds of dollars became recklessly squandered on dinners and birthdays.

High on the Yellow Spur, her hair was soaked by the rain, as though we had bathed together. But underneath that coy shell was a beastliness...a wild woman....

Crows spoke to us. A pigeon fluttered near my head by the ridge where I stood on a small foothold belaying. His tiny red eyes... for him too, Eldorado was egg, nest, home, and Louvre — place of surprise, art, and views.

On top of the wall, I found and fed my pediatrician wild raspberries which made her pucker, her inner mouth wet, decorative, inlaid with mythical and allegorical themes. After all my ranting, after the mother goose confessions and gypsy moth flutterings, the Eldorado cryptography boils down to a woman's hair rising and blowing in the storm.

She went away almost as quickly, as harshly, as she had appeared. Somehow, somewhere, for some reason...we were apart, to continue in new respective oblivions of our lives, with only memories.

Winter was a time of uncertainty and repentance, though being still one with her anatomy and eyes, hearing in my mind laughter and Leonard Cohen music.... The canyon became lonely for me. I sat on the point of a rock near the river. I wondered if I could climb the Yellow Spur again.

How many years have I been pricked by the illustrious flower Eldorado, scratched by its tiny barbs and holds....

80 Lbs

In the early seventies, I was approached by a small boy whose name was Jeff Schwenn, eighty pounds, about four and a half feet tall, thirteen years old, blond hair, pale. He sent me a letter expressing a desire to meet me.

He was a chronic asthmatic, I learned, an illness which had prevented him from functioning in normal vigorous activities of youth. But now he was attracted to climbing.

He was straightforward, unpretentious, with insight and rapport beyond his years. I learned from him the game of chess. With a frail snicker he looked up through the top of his glasses and pronounced mate.

The month we met, I had a girlfriend who was unfortunately an alcoholic. Jeff stopped by one day to visit me and waited in the living room as I finished taking a shower. He noticed a large bottle of tequila my girlfriend had left sitting on a table. After three or four minutes it took to emerge from the bathroom, I heard a tiny laugh and saw an empty bottle standing where one had previously been full. He exhibited an innocent stillness. He had guzzled the bitter poison fast and straight. Half what he consumed would have flown me out windows. He was smiling, paralyzed, trying to find me with his eyes, a horrible vaporized look across his face.

In climbing, no one ever seemed more ready to do the impossible. At intervals, he would pull a device from his pocket and spray something down his throat. I was uncertain whether he should be climbing at all. He spoke of having to go to the hospital, for shots of adrenalin — treatment for radical asthma.

But the adrenalin which occurred in him naturally as we climbed on warm Eldorado days miraculously stimulated breathing!

His doctor and parents were amazed by the effect of the new medicine. He was invited to give a slide show on climbing at the National Center for Asthma Research, in Denver.

In Eldorado, I resourcefully lifted his eighty pounds high above my head to clip the rope through a fixed anchor which otherwise would have required a couple of scary moves to reach.

He taught me to water ski.

He wrote in a short climbing article, "Before meeting Pat, I heard that he is egotistical. After getting to know him, however, I find that he is."

To spark excitement in him, I placed him on some difficult climbs, inadvertently scaring myself.

The wind caught his light body while making a long free rappel off the Maiden Spire south of Boulder. He was blown into a long slow swing on the rope through frightening space.

I wanted to see his adrenalin rush.

Gray

I think of seventeen-year-old Gray Ringsby who I started climbing with in 1979 when he was thirteen—a little bit feeble and vacant then, but receptive.

In 1983 he is lean, delicate, sound, and unconcerned. I am twice his age, but there exists a polarization—a two-way learning experience where we merge neither as mentor nor student but somewhere between.

A mood of adventure is evoked in me by a fresh and new friend, an accelerating drive in him imperious to my eccentricities.

"I'm really beginning to feel thirsty and tired," I say.

"No you're not."

He is never overly molded. Neither is he, in turn, manipulative.

He climbs a desperate finger-tip crack his first try which takes me several tries to duplicate.

Some individuals have upon occasion supposed I climb with younger people because they are easily controlled, over-powered by my character in some dominating way, allowing me to be the leader and to exert my ego. Fearing such observations might have even the slightest modicum of truth, I check it out directly with Gray.

"Do you feel that I dominate and control you?"

The answer does not come immediately, but a little later, unexpectedly while climbing.

"I really hate it, Pat, when you make me wear that spiked dog collar."

I am reluctant to compliment him at the end of the day.

"I'm proud of you, Gray, you really did a good job."

"Yes, but I couldn't have made it without...(putting a hand on my shoulder)...my basic skill and technique."

In late rays of light and strength we hike downward in a forest.

"Pat, do you want to go bouldering tomorrow? Or are you too old and brittle?"

Some of the newer climbs are too hard for me. I might be able to get up them somehow...I mean with a little direct aid, or maybe if I was shot out of a cannon or something. 5.12 exists, but I am not quite yet imbued with its significance. Upward progress is made in degrees and fractions...metaphysical hints. Eldorado is beautiful, the light diffused, bands of sun to the west the colors of the spectrum.

Gray and I are right for one another — an even balance of personalities. I hold him back slightly, with my specialized climbing interests — his desire is to consume all climbs in sight. There is vitality, a brightness, a happiness fixed upon his countenance. On a trip together to Yosemite in spring, 1983, he is at the center of my life for three weeks. A long winter has left me stressed and irritated. With Gray, the stress lifts. Quoting a Bob Dylan song, he says,

"Okay, Mr. 'I know you've suffered much,' let's go climbing."

Resting an elbow on my shoulder, he observes, "This is another fine mess you've gotten us into Ollie." I am envious of his youth which seems more humble, perceptive, organized, and relaxed than was mine.

For many years I have struggled somewhat awkwardly in climbing, writing, photography, film, and music to crystalize the feelings of my heart. Finally, in a great disillusionment, there comes a breakthrough, a sweet, quiet realization that, with Gray, the climbing doesn't even really seem to exist. I am rather caught in the expanding influence of obscurity, of loneliness, of ego death, in the power of a pure, beloved comrade — valuable, important — a friend who is there as I go up and as I go down.

The Toe

On a climb in Eldorado in the late sixties, a friend, John Lewis, was momentarily standing on a ledge when a rock the size of a refrigerator inopportunely became unglued and slid a couple of feet downward, stopping precariously directly in front of him. It gently balanced at an angle, pinning his big toe to the ledge.

Miraculously the toe was not crushed flat but was simply held there.

John remained still, assuming the slightest whimper or movement would send the rock sliding more. There was nothing to do but call for help. His belayer found a traverse off, and the rescue group was alerted. I too was called.

Several of us ascended to the ledge where John silently stood. We speculated on strategies.

"Now this is the rock we have to be careful of," the rescue leader said, giving it a big slap. John's eyes nearly flew out of their sockets, though he remained motionless and quiet.

The big rock was finally tied off and hoisted an inch upward, off the valuable toe.

The Professor

In the late seventies, a distinguished professor of government from the University of Washington phoned and arranged for a climb with me in summer. I pride myself in safe, meaningful rock climbing instruction. But after twenty or more years as a guide and teacher, it can get old. I must work at keeping my interest in it. Varied settings provide diversity. On a short granite wall, in fits of falling, toes fixed, the professor's heels bounced up and down while his knees waved laterally.

After the route, we found ourselves bushwhacking in poison ivy. The river was near, offering relief and across which was a short cut to the car. We waded to our thighs, then to our chests. I underestimated the depth and swiftness of the river. Inching outward irreversibly into the deepening channel, I noticed my scholar was not present. Had he momentarily gone fishing? I grabbed for a coiled rope which had hung from his shoulder and now was surfacing. I pulled hard on the coils. He bobbed up, spewing water. I held one of his hands to give him stability. The current pushed and shoved us across, as we took short steps downstream. But now our course led unavoidably to a previously unnoticed, topless nymph cavorting in our path on the far bank. She perched in the sun, a little poetic jewel, uninhibited by my client's befuddled glances and disintegrating composure. He wallowed in a shallow eddy, laden with sopping equipment, water pouring from his pants, holding my hand.

Buildering

The activity of bouldering is given city vernacular as a rock climber manifests himself on convenient brick walls, window ledges, pillars, doorjambs. A church provides not only good buildering but sanctuary in the event of police. Shingles, drainpipes, aerials make good holds—when they don't tear off.

As a teenager, a "buildering" place was Boulder High School after dark. Without sight, one needed a sense of feel, balance futile. A non-climber convinced himself one night he could match my moves. We began up the side of the school. Near the top, with a slip likely to be fatal, he leaned—oozed—backward suddenly off the wall. By a fluke, his hand fell onto—happened around—a thin metal fixture protruding from the wall. His body swung there, life preserved by a simple stroke of fate.

In the hippie era of the mid-later sixties, there was a sort of revolution going on around Colorado between the cops and the freaks. Someone had hidden a bomb under a parked police car, so the authorities stationed police officers with rifles as snipers atop a couple of buildings surrounding the Boulder police station. I was not radical enough to be a hippie and not straight enough to cry over a blown police car, but I enjoyed buildering. A friend and I attempted one night to ascend the city library. It closely flanked the Boulder police station and had on its roof, unbeknownst to us, a sniper. A flagstone wall ran out, and fifteen feet of smooth concrete continued to the top. My friend stood on my shoulders, then in my hands, as I attempted to press his weight vertically. He stretched to within an inch of the summit, unaware of any hidden presence above.

After a few tries we descended, a day later discovering—through an acquaintance who worked for the police—that two freaks had come an inch from being sacrificed as examples.

For all the hazards in buildering there were rewards. Moved by an impulse to climb the underside of a stairway in a crowded mall, with about a dozen onlookers quickly gathering, a girlfriend experienced her skirt unbutton and fall off. It would have been a minor thing had she worn the slightest undergarment.

Tom Ruwitch and I walked inside Norlin Library on the University of Colorado campus, to escape a rainy day, and found a crack to climb formed by a plaster pillar against a wall. Tom wedged a side of his body in and started upward. A peculiar looking man appeared, standing still with a briefcase, suit, and glasses. I had heard stories of bizarre people inhabiting the library and had once been watched through a small hole in the restroom, so I tried to ignore the person now gazing oppressively at us. My partner grabbed a small ledge formed by the top of the pillar. The ledge unexpectedly disintegrated in hand, sending several fragments of plaster noisily to the floor. The third party gave us an effeminate sort of wave of the wrist and blurted in a falsetto,

"I'm telling!"

He hurried down the stairs. For awhile we hid ourselves in the labyrinth of the library. It was not an easy matter, with conspicuous white climbing pants and orange cagoules, to finally sneak out. They waited for us at the door. Tom went first and said I did it. I came later and said he did it.

In the early seventies I worked on a demolition crew, hired to help destroy a three story building—by hand. The foreman had a brainstorm of hiring rock climbers who would be unintimidated by danger or height! I recognized other climbers who also found themselves charmed by the fifteen dollars an hour wage. Not one of us possessed the slightest good sense or know-how at destroying buildings, including the boss. This was his first demolition.

And so the building began to fall apart from the foundation up. I was a little incredulous as a brick flew past my head from two stories above. To my horror, people tore at the very floors which held together the sides. We hammered things right out from under ourselves and tight-roped along beams. Brick walls balanced precariously in the wind, stripped of their props.

About mid-day the boss and I both fell suddenly through a ceiling, learning that dry-wall bears only the illusion it will support one. Death is nature's way of saying that you are in pain. Or so I thought, landing (fortunately) on a narrow crossbeam.

Montage

A seventh-grader attracted to the rocks above Boulder, Colorado, I set out one day with Susie—a Springer spaniel. Climbing equipment consisted of a large link chain—something I found in the corner of a shed. I could not yet envision how such a chain might be used. But it looked to be a device one could fasten some way to a rock.

Thus I began, intrigued, full of schemes. I had faith the challenges would dictate the techniques. The chain had to be discarded somewhere in the forest well below, cumbersome, heavy, jingly, too long. Higher on the rock, only a dog knew how to climb. The ten feet I did gain seemed hard. We retreated, happy, confused, as spontaneously as we had begun. The chain probably remains there, rusting in the talus to this day, a curious remnant of bold explorations of the past.

A hemp rope ran through little posts around a fraternity house lawn. Members of the fraternity sat in chairs on the porch. No one paid particular attention to a small boy sitting near. Nor was I noticed sawing with a knife. I cut through a knot which held my first climbing rope there. Then, in anticipation of being chased, I boldly ran, holding the end of the rope in hand. A hundred feet of rope trailed full length behind, sliding on the sidewalk, down a street, up an alley. No one ever followed.

In ninth grade I found a mesa in Boulder above a residential street in the middle of town. A climb was done up ninety feet of near-vertical dirt, an ice axe used to cut steps, dirt clods raining on pedestrians below.

In a field near my parents' Boulder home, I mastered several overhanging trees—pitons hammered directly into the bark.

In 1959, on a five dollar bet with a gas station attendant, I climbed the most awesome, precarious tree on the university campus but was later denied the five when it was learned I used a rope.

As early teenagers, Larry Dalke and I had a number of fiascos. Before sunrise one dark morning we approached the flatiron rocks above Boulder and, along the way, stopped and cooked breakfast in the forest. We carefully put out the fire with pine needles. From high on the third flatiron, we monitored the progress of a small forest fire in the vicinity of where we had cooked a pre-dawn meal. It did not occur to us who started the blaze (which was fortunately squelched by volunteers from Boulder).

Larry and I were chased in the foothills by a cow. With heavy packs on, it was difficult to run away.

We were once stranded high on the flatirons with only starlight, laughing, crying, whimpering, praying, shivering into the stone. How we got ourselves down eludes memory.

Larry and I were members of a small band and, during a break in a performance, quickly drove up one night to nearby Flagstaff Mountain. We free-soloed a ninety-foot wall in the dark in dress shoes and suits.

On the walls of Eldorado an afternoon when I was learning to lead, I ascended a short distance, became scared, and returned. Ready to employ all resources, I asked my partner, Steve Komito, for his shoes. We changed shoes on a ledge, and I moved upward again — to be defeated at the same place.

As a neophyte climber, one day I could not find my piton hammer. I took the first hammer found in my father's tool shop. Sixty feet up a steep balance climb, at the first opportunity for a piton to be placed, I discovered the hammer was made of lead. One stroke cut a piton impression in the mushy metal.

At age fourteen, I fell off a boulder after dark. Larry spotted from below. As I reached the top, he lost interest and walked a few feet away. It was then I became disoriented in the night. From about fifteen feet up, I was on the ground sprawled unevenly across the dirt...face up. The moon was moving in a strange, wide circle. Attempting but unable to conceal my anguish I stood up quickly, attempting to say "Nice catch." But the wind was completely knocked out of me — that horrible gasping feeling, uncertain as to whether you will breathe again. My mouth opened, yet for several frustrating seconds it was impossible to speak.

Learning to rappel was traumatic, with no instruction outside of a filling-station attendant who described the technique as running the rope around my bottom. He wasn't exactly sure—maybe it was between the legs and over a shoulder. I gave myself a rather frantic hot-seat on a few occasions attempting to master the procedure out of trees and off the roof of my parents' house, the rope wrapped around the square knife-edges of a small, teetering brick chimney. I once tried feeding the rope through my belt loops. If all else failed, I could simply go down hand over hand...and several times did.

I was too busy trying to unravel these mysteries of climbing technique to realize I suffered from acute acrophobia. When the right way to use rope and carabiners in a rappel was finally learned, half way down a rock I went crackers—in a silent sort of way, suddenly freezing, motionless on a small ledge. It took a gentle man in his late fifties, Baker Armstrong, to happen by and help me pry my fingers from around the rope.

The wild and famous sixties brought to brew a strange seething-pot of energy and personality. Bob Dylan sang on the radio and captured the imagination. My climbing friend Dave Rearick fed me protein powder and taught me gymnastic presses.

Tall and awesome Layton Kor was on the scene, storming the Eldorado walls. He was a bricklayer by profession, on a few horror climbs causing me to lay some bricks of my own.

Climbers occasionally admonished me for excessive reference to myself. I needed only to be heard. And so was I heard: recognition of my faults was total and immediate.

Layton phoned from the Longs Peak ranger station and said to come and be on his support party for his ascent of the Diamond Wall with Royal Robbins. I had no transportation, so Kor said to go to his house in Boulder, get his Ford, and drive it. I agreed, wanting to be a part of the adventures. It seemed three small points that I had no driver's license, did not know how to drive, and was under age. Layton didn't ask. I didn't volunteer the information. I drove toward Longs Peak, trying to learn to shift, confusing brake and clutch, jerking to a stop, killing the engine at stoplights, squealing the tires, finally side-swiping a car in the narrow road within a hundred yards of the Longs Peak ranger station and telling the driver that I was Layton Kor. I did not tell Layton about the loss of paint and metal on one side of his car, for fear it would ruin his climb.

In the mid-sixties, special permission and a hard hat were required to climb on Devil's Tower in Wyoming. I was forced to wear a ranger's hard hat which had a bill protruding out of the front of it. This made it difficult to keep from falling over backwards off the climb. It was necessary to climb with my head turned to one side.

A rock the size of a Greyhound bus fell past Larry Dalke and me while doing the third ascent of the diagonal route on Longs Peak in about 1965. We rappelled off and returned with hard hats!

In 1966, Roger Raubach and I were forced to bivouac at thirteen thousand feet on Longs Peak with no coats and only one sweater. For food, we had two tiny cherry life-savers. The next day, Roger had to leave his camera for gas in the town of Lyons.

One day on the Crack of Fear I wore two different types of climbing shoes—a Cortina on the right foot, Kronhoeffer on the left. One was better for crack technique and the other better for face holds on the wall outside the crack.

...Paul Mayrose had a cat that ate only cheese and rubber bands. You could drop that cat, and it would land on its back.

On the rim of the Black Canyon an afternoon while walking with a ranger, I flew out of my shoes when I almost stepped on the largest rattle snake I had seen. The ranger reached down and picked up the snake in his hand!

"Only a Gopher snake," he said, "completely harmless, but they imitate the rattlesnake for protection." The snake, detected as a fraud, became docile, a look of dejection on its face. An incriminating fat bulge in the snake's middle was evidence it had recently glutted on a rodent. I thought I detected in the snake's face a look of guilt. It waited patiently to be set down to go about the business of scaring people and swallowing things.

...In a hair-crackling electrical storm while climbing in Eldorado in the sixties I said to my fourteen-year-old partner Roger Briggs, "Let's get out of here, it's lightning." Roger observed, "Well, isn't this rock grounded?"

While leading an overhanging wall on Longs Peak in the early sixties, a piton I was hanging from fell out. As I flew through the air, my belayer—hidden under a projection of rock and unable to see me—yelled,

"You don't have to yank it. I'll give you slack."

In Yosemite in the early sixties, I learned one must be responsible for oneself:

"I'll take care of the bivouac food, you bring some pitons," Chris Fredericks said. On a hot evening bivouac a thousand feet up Sentinel Rock, he pulled out our rations for two days: an orange, a candy bar, a piece of cheese.

Royal Robbins made the first solo ascent of El Capitan in Yosemite in the late sixties and spent ten days alone on the three thousand-foot wall. One afternoon Liz, Royal's wife, and I went to the meadow below El Cap to try to spot Royal. He was high on the great wall, appearing as only a tiny red dot—even through a small pair of binoculars Liz had brought. We silently stared upward, struggling to fixate on him. Liz strained to hold the binoculars still enough to capture the red dot. She quietly gazed upward, in awe, at the granite oblivion. Suddenly she said, "Good move, Royal."

Tom Ruwitch was seventeen and I twenty when we made the tenth ascent of the nose of El Capitan in 1967 in about three and a half days. We could have done the route in about two days had we not spent as much time lapsing into comas on ledges from July heat. We both lost about twenty pounds in three days, as emaciated as vampires. The first thing we did after the climb was go to Yosemite Lodge and down two rootbeer floats apiece. Recovering from the climb was minor by comparison.

Trying to hitch-hike home from Yosemite that summer, Tom and I found ourselves in Winnemucca, Nevada, one of the forsaken nowheres of the western United States. Hitch-hiking was outlawed, but we were permitted to walk several miles outside of town...where cars moved at hyper-space. Here, trying to catch a ride amused the police. The desert heat incinerated us. Finally we adopted a strategy where Tom took one side of the road hitchhiking west and I took the opposite side going east. After several hours, a car stopped. Here were two Wyoming climbers on their way to Yosemite. We didn't argue. I finally said that Yosemite was unbearably hot, and climbers were leaving. To my surprise, this observation caused the driver to turn the car around immediately and, without discussion, burn rubber in an easterly direction. I might just as soon have said his hub caps had fallen off.

One afternoon in the Yosemite climber's campground Pratt meandered by. He sat down across from me at a picnic table and placed before us a newly purchased repellent device—a small, round, scented pellet designed to attract and then poison flies. He had a sinister grin, as though looking for some perverse entertainment on a hot day. We waited silently. At last, a large fly landed on the table, took a drink from the pellet and paused. You could feel the anticipation, Pratt hovering over the pellet and fly, hoping for results. Suddenly the fly stood up on a hind leg and began to spin like a ballerina. It stopped, and then...dropped dead. Pratt glanced slowly up at me, repulsed, delighted, and slowly walked away shaking his head.

In the middle of the night in one of the Yosemite campgrounds, I heard clanging sounds outside the tent. I had forgotten to put away a box of canned goods. Ruwitch was sleeping in a hammock between two trees about a hundred feet away, with several other climbers. I recognized his voice:

"Ha ha, the bears got Pat's camp."

A few seconds later, the same voice came in a different tone: "Shoo bear."

Royal Robbins, his wife Liz, and I shared a spaghetti dinner in Moab, Utah, camped and bouldered in Arches National Monument, hiked and played, living out of a Mercedes. A windshield wiper broke in a downpour, and the car got stuck in deep, red desert mud while we were lost on a back road. Royal and I found ourselves covered with mud from stacking rocks under the wheels. Royal pulled the car up to a cow standing dumbly alongside the road and asked for directions.

We coasted twenty miles to a gas station in Moab.

The three of us finished Utah's Castleton Tower (the third ascent of the spire in 1964) at dusk, and rappelled the five hundred or more feet from the summit in blackness. Royal almost seemed to plan the benightings, for added adventure or to eliminate the exposure of desert rappels.

Royal, Liz, and I descended in the dark from Shiprock, down two thousand feet in the night. A ghostly New Mexico wind blew admonishing voices at us. Stars of the desert lit the way to a midnight steak dinner we cooked below. We were oblivious to time.

Seventeen hundred feet above the ground, near the top of the Diamond in a storm in 1964, Bob Boucher whispered, "Be brave." As I moved above, he slowly dissolved before my eyes into a cloud of snow.

A little story for change of pace, make of it what you will:

While helping give a climbing seminar with Royal in Salt Lake City in 1964, I met a climber—seventeen years old, as I too was then—by the name of Mark Maquarrie. The friendship seemed instant. A warmth pervaded everyone he touched. Some months later, in Boulder, I was awakened from a bad dream. The dream did not make sense. I saw the Diamond wall of Longs Peak, and in its center were four letters: M-A-R-K. The only Mark I knew was my friend in Salt Lake. A few weeks later, I received a letter from Mike Covington who planned to climb the Diamond with me soon. In the letter, Mike said our mutual friend, Mark Maquarrie, had been killed climbing...and that we should name the proposed new route on the Diamond the Mark Maquarrie Wall!

In 1975 David Breashears persuaded me to go to Yosemite, determined to get me in shape after a long layoff. I was privileged to share a part of his life where he was a teen and in incredible rock climbing shape. He was practically possessed, ascending severe pitches with daring and speed. On the other hand, I was a besotted chess casualty recovering from a sort of psychic murder, chess played eight hours a day for about a year, physical conditioning sacrificed like a pawn. He made me exercise: pullups on tree limbs, pushups, situps in the campground.... Denied food, I was caught sneaking into a can of spaghetti.

I had to really push to climb near his league. We teamed up with Jim Erickson for a two pitch climb up a difficult crack on a Yosemite formation called The Cookie. About a hundred or more feet up, we reached a comfortable ledge. Next Jim belayed the young dynamo up a desperate lieback called Catchey Corner. David sped quickly above us. I walked along the ledge and sat fifteen feet to the side of Jim, enjoying the scenery. A psychic impulse called me back toward Jim. Jim noticed with curiosity as my hands reached for the belay rope which led to David. I grabbed the red line and pulled it a second after David accidentally fell over backwards and began sailing through the air. Together Erickson and I were able to create the right dynamic belay, bringing David to a slow stop from a lone piece of protection he had placed: a no. 1 hexentric nut with five-mil. Perlon, a tiny piece of aluminum and thin cord separating a simple mistake from a hundred and fifty-foot ground fall. I cannot explain what prompted me to come over and take part in the belaying of the rope.

The only relaxation found with David in Yosemite was play-ing the piano evenings in the lodge. Even here he cut me little slack. After a few minutes at the piano, as I began to warm up, he said nervously, "Play one more and we'll go." His intensity seemed almost to disturb his mind, activating him in his sleep. One night he leaped out of his sleeping bag and threw rocks at a tree he was dreaming was a bear.

About five years later, a much calmer David Breashears wrote in a letter to me,

"Don't let the young Eldorado hot shots get too swelled up. I guess you must forgive them. They forget whose shoulders they are standing on to see the horizons of today."

In 1980, while making a film with Tom Frost of Tom Higgins and Christian Griffith in Tuolumne, Frost and I climbed a route running parallel to the climb we filmed. I tied into a rope and led over a bulge to a long crack which I ascended. A heavy tape recorder hung from my neck, choking the feeling out of my right arm and fingers. I was moving slow and carefully, fearing the recorder might throw me off at any time, when all at once Frost, my supposed belayer, was climbing a few feet directly behind me. He had run out of patience.

On a sunny afternoon in the mid-seventies, John Gill and I ascended together unroped up a five hundred-foot granite buttress west of Pueblo, Colorado. At a short difficult section over great exposure John pulled from a waist pack a thirty-foot clothesline rope and lowered an end of it to belay me.

"Is this rope any good?" I asked.

"Oh yes. I bought it at K-Mart just the other day."

In Yosemite in about 1980, John Bachar had a pair of dark glasses with a tiny hidden red light attached behind the center of each frame, lights which blinked on or off as he so decided by pushing a little button he held in his pocket. Apparently the button was connected to the lights by a small concealed wire which ran out an arm of the glasses and inconspicuously down to his pocket. At night he was sometimes found standing mysteriously outside the lodge and looking in, like a racoon, or he was sitting in the lodge, in a lurking way, half nodding, hoping for an elderly tourist couple to glance indifferently at him at which instant his eyes would blink on and off, along with a sinister smile, leaving the couple dumbstruck.

Playing chess in the lodge one evening, I glanced up after making a move and saw John watching from outside. His eyes blinked approval, little lights of victory telegraphing through a window.

1980. Driving through Yosemite, I am pulled over by the rangers. Going a little slow, scanning the surrounding rocks and lush valley, I have supposedly swerved. The rangers tell me to keep my eyes on the road.

1977. Bill Briggs. I am awed by an effortless way in which he persuades holds to tumble into a graceful accommodation. A drop of rain produces fear. A difficult crack shreds our hands. My quasimodo friend questions his newly acquired Ph.D. During a rest between climbs, we nap sitting in the front seat of the car. A fly buzzes into Bill's mouth and out again....

I was never the best climber but had flares — a few right places at the right time. If I had lived in Kansas.... Had I been born in the Renaissance...or as a Laplander.... If I had been anyone else or anywhere else I would not have known the climbs, opportunities, teachers, students, and friends I did. How many climbers can say they learned under the wing of Robbins, in the shadow of Kor, in the osmosis of Gill, touched by the light of Higgins and spirit of Frost?

In 1980 in Yosemite, I rose up about five feet, lifted suddenly by a large, loud earthquake rippling through the meadow where I sat. Rumor was that climbing nuts and pitons fell out, as cracks widened. Two quakes hit that day, the second while I was attending a little church service in the small chapel below Sentinel Rock. We slid laterally back and forth, from one end of our pews to the other, listening to the solo performance of a woman vocalist who the Bishop later complimented for providing an earth-shaking rendition.

Somewhere in all of the climbs and human fronts is trapped a person. In the many swashbuckling memories was he sealed, in reality, to a more simple route, less obvious?

After committing myself in 1977 to a spiritual path, John Gill wrote, "Well, old friend, I'm happy to hear that you took the leap of faith. Climbing, really, is only a symptom of a deeper quest, and those who are fortunate continue to grow and seek."

With a certain dangerous disregard for rushing in where angels fear to tread, a climber asked the very straight Tom Frost if he wanted to go get a bottle of Bailey's Irish Cream. Tom replied, "What for? I don't see any ships to christen."

Climbing is clear. We climb and spiral, laugh, and rise again, a little serious, a bit cynical....

Royal was impressed with a sign in Yosemite which read, "Exfoliating granite." Maestros, maelstroms....

Perhaps someone will dream my name on the side of a wall.

The following article appeared in Mountain Magazine, June 1986. Climbers everywhere, it seemed, were becoming ludicrous in their search for higher number gradings and for equipment sponsors. It was the dawn of power bolt drills, in an attempt to reduce every last pristine rock surface to a state of climbability—whatever the style. In the same spirit, Ronald Reagan declared one day on television, "No glory is too great."

I appreciated the athleticism of rock climbers but believed that there was much more to be felt than just that. Rather than looking for bigger and bigger successes, one needed to become larger in their perception of beauty and detail.

No Glory is Too Small

Suffering a breakdown in judgment, I started up the "Crack of Fear" in Rocky Mountain National Park. Thor was already sending thunder, and there was an occasional, sickening flash of lightning. Wind flew up the long, slender crack, up my pantlegs, into my shirt, and through my hair. There was something wonderful about being electrified.

If I were to let go I would fall out of the crack and drop fifteen vertical feet before there could be any chance of the rope catching me. My rope ran through one or two marginal points I had set below. It was a sinking feeling to hear my belayer, who stood below, say it would be okay if I didn't want to do this climb.

I moved upward with a combination of cow grunts and surgical cunning. At one move, the chances of my not slipping were as good as trying to touch the cornea of the eye without triggering a blink. I was no longer a cherub of the 1960's. Years of spaghetti poisoning and recent weeks of sloth had accelerated a loss of commitment.

I encountered a sling and a carabiner - shrapnel left by other climbers who had wisely retreated.

One day I read in a newspaper how someone at a football game suddenly turned and stabbed a total stranger sitting next to him. Asked why he had done it, he replied, "He was trying to steal my sexual magnetic rays." For me, that one statement seemed to capture the flying apart of much of modern life. The world was becoming sick, and I along with it. We were victims of data imposed on us by competition. The world was drifting deeper into bad intellectual habits. Even rock climbing was becoming muddled in jealousies, cross-generational conflicts, confused self-appraisals, and ruminations about ethics. What was happening to the good spirit of climbing?

I personally was disposed to a certain psychic damage — as a result of years of exposure?

We seemed less in need of the acceptance of our climbing peers. I contemplated Edmund Burke's suggestion that admiration and respect are inferior effects.

We began to imperil climbing by over-indulging in comparison - speculation as to who is the best climber or what the hardest route is. Each new jolt of high climbing gradings is like the last jerk of a corpse, a dead idea, a hope ad nauseam. "Progress," as signified by rising number grades, has never been an indicator of character, intelligence, or advance. The aura of gradings has been diluted by three decades of climbing. Somewhere the mystique was fated to depart, beginning where gradings were first used as weapons of one-upmanship.

It is very easy to talk of another climber's failure or success when its reality is a safe distance from your own experience. The difficulty of climbing must not be taken as equivalent to the statement of climbing. Difficulty does not give climbing its force, but climbing gives difficulty a force.

There have always been climbers proficient at technical difficulty. Relative to each time period, climbers are no more creative now than they ever were. Yet there will always exist the mental air castles of "standard setting." The values, terms, starting points, goals, experience, and physical attributes of climbers are never equal, a knowledge without which climbing becomes pathetically amateurish. Rock climbing is personal search in a reality where one step higher or harder is not necessarily one step nearer to things. Indeed a summit, or the solution to a sequence on rock, can be a type of tragic discovery.

The pathos of climbing, therefore, must be found in its self-surrender, in the desire, for example, that many routes remain unclimbed, that a host of "unknowns" be willed to the heights to inspire us, to signal our temporal ways, to limit our glory. Where is the wonder of a climbing lead when it is previewed or pre-bolted by rappel?

The climber's theology—at last refined—is the execution of non-performance.

The short, gritstone routes of Britain bear more significance for me than an ascent of Everest or the Eiger North Wall in winter. This is because these small crags were never thought of as "ultimate." In the conquest of the "impossible," one can only encounter a great insufficiency. There is no elite climb that will not eventually be visited by circuses. I am content to climb an old favorite route, upward, free, away from TV evangelists.

Climbing can be a type of poetry. Years of eelish verticalities can be compressed into a few coherent steps, a small number of basic movements which call to memory—in sensory replay—the best of all that has gone before or the best that is capable of happening. Whether the climbing be moderate or exacting, the movement is the same. A leg pushes upward, balance is required. The materials are the same—rock, sunlight, thought. Climbing is rooted deep in the body. It is gratifying, amusing, healthy to climb. There is pleasure in a drop of water, or an obscure boulder never visited before.

Climbing is earthy, with tones of science fiction, freaky, weird, compelling. A person is moved out of society and thrown into exaggerated relief. "Childhood," a poet once wrote, "is a kingdom where nobody dies." Another poet stated that the difference between old age and youth is that you no longer think that you are divine. The sociologist observes that we progress in stages of cognitive development—each stage qualitatively more experienced than the preceding ones. Is this true in climbing? One day I found myself solo climbing in the rain. Fifty feet above the ground I was struck with a sense of self-worth in the face of finitude. Climbing had evolved toward more and more risk. I did not want to become one of the body count, a line of impersonal corpses. As I climbed, my imagination considered the ghoulish symbolism of soloing. I thought of television commercials which used climbing. I thought of the pressure on the young to earn respect through solo climbing. It seemed tragic that to achieve status one should have to put his life near the edge, inspired by a lethal pecking order. By the time a climber grows up, he is so addicted to this necromania of the climbing culture that its constant cultivation seems to provide for him a morbid sense of normalcy.

Slowly society lessens its dependence upon one's contributions, as though society were preparing one for that ultimate form of social disengagement. One realizes that climbing is not a contest, it is an accumulation. A sense of wholeness can be found by a climber looking back at all that he has done, fulfillment found in a transcendent frame of reference. The philosopher Pascal stated, "There is a God-shaped vacuum in the heart of each man."

A climber can begin again toward wholeness at the crux which turns him back. A few rents in his armor, but his mind has profited. Perception has been sharpened. Like creating music, in listening to the music as it forms, in listening to it for what IT says it needs, the climber, the composer, the vacuum which seeks fulfillment, listens, feels, waits, watches for what climbing needs.

Redgarden Wall, in Eldorado Canyon, Colorado, seems to tip, or to break up, to lean slightly under a moving cloud. The total perceptual effect is one of activity, of power, something living. Such effects come in part from one's orientation to vertical and horizontal lines. Climbing is a departure from orientations. Quiet, unbroken areas of the wall pull a climber's attention. Cracks create lines, faces are lines between lines. Twisting, overlapping slabs of rock. Contrasting yellows of the stone. Near the end of the day the sky conforms in color to the rock.

The wall appears to expand, or to contract. An eye may emphasize or deny mass, depending on mood, weather, or wind. The wall may seem hard, lifeless, impenetrable, a convergence of strange, anatomical forms, spurs, with blocklike permanence, or it may possess a softness in round, displaced corners. A swallow suddenly dives. There is an order to these spaces. The order is approached through the fingertips. There are textures of the rock—rough, slick, the concavity of the holds as opposed to the sharpness of their edges. A small groove has been shined for centuries by rain. Color alters, a green flows where there were yellows. Blue, orange. It is astounding that there is no color at all, rather that one's eyes receive the information of light, and the brain attributes a color.

The chemistries of the natural world are the mother science, the deeper law. Silence, solar system, soil, the taste of wild raspberries, little reeds of rock, fingerholds. To climb is to be nurtured - life, joy, friendship, light, and these countered by their opposites, deadness, suffering, alienation, darkness. Alongside beginnings there exist ends, the ends of lives, end of youth, ends of climbs. These paired opposites, as in literature, are the contrasts by which a climber feels. We tend to lose the opposites in climbing when we think "up" only.

The "phenomenology" of climbing - given moments - examines fresh the instant of life. As in film, the mind remembers quick impressions, sensory arousals encoded into the depth of memory, a series of bristling equilibria - opposing and self-competing forces. The mind will later produce these moves as dreams, to satisfy, fulfill, study, or refine.

It is amazing that a mind can bring fingers and feet precisely to a set of minute holds. Vision strives for improvement of body position. Sense organs in the joints and muscles send signals to the brain to indicate the position of the joints and the degree of tension in the muscles. Equilibratory sense begins at the semicircular canals and vestibular sacs of the inner ear. The semicircular canals, oriented at right angles to one another, are filled with fluid that moves as the person's head rotates or the position of his body changes. Cells in the ear trigger neurons toward the brain. The right hemisphere of the brain is responsible for spatial relationships. And so on, one experiences the power of being kinesthetically in balance.

The mind is fed by an enriched environment. A psychological study once examined jewel fish and found that fish placed in an "enriched" environment, with stimulation and variety, had far greater development of certain glia cells and dendritic branchings associated with intelligence.

The imposing crags of England poke up from misty heather. A sweep of blond Yosemite granite rises huge, hot. One learns of his smallness at the foot of El Capitan. Above Yosemite, slabs of Tuolumne flash with glacier polish like Indian messages sent by mirror. Enormous, gray buttresses are enshrouded by the deep, mysterious Black Canyon of Colorado. The red, lonely sandstone spires of the Utah desert teeter against sun and wind. A climber must crawl through barbed wire fence to skin-slicing Split Rocks near Estes Park. Colorado's Diamond Face on Longs Peak seems to overhang slightly for a thousand feet. Here one ascends in an exotic corridor between dripping water and sheer wall. The slender, wind-lashed Crack of Fear brings tense moves, as hail stings the fingers. A climber disappears into a cloud high on a Dolomite wall, his countenance shaped by storm and lichen as though it had been dipped into a bowl of pesto.

After a long, cross-country drive, a ten-foot high boulder becomes a celestial Venus. A climber is one who finds climbing where you put him, alert acceptance of the most sedate outcrops. Bouldering does not lack the beauty or valor of alpinism. In bouldering one is able to transcend the dementia of "porta-ledges" and rappel-placed bolts.

The Crack of Fear blackened in the shadows of clouds. I thought of England and the rainy climbs of Don Whillans. As my body seemed to sink downward in the crack, at a moment of low self esteem, I recalled how much Don meant to me. This was a friendship, as others, which had found its resonating image in climbing. Climbing bears no greater significance than how it reappears in mutual thought as a new and higher fact.

Within a hundred feet I had employed most of the basic techniques of climbing - an edge move, a handjamb, an arm-lock, a heel-and-toe jamb. There was a brief lieback, a traverse, a short bit of face climbing, an off-width move, a stem. Higher, the route would present an undercling, a flared chimney, and a mantel. It was my favorite climb in part because of this variety but in part because the moves continued to remain within my ability. Like Supremacy Crack and Country Club Crack near Boulder, the Crack of Fear could be done again and again and not cease to bring pleasure. I had done the climb five or six times during the previous ten years and had not, through familiarity, encountered a lessening of excitement. It occurred to me that one does not leave his mark on a climb, as though to place a name on a tomb to insure some perpetuation. Stone rather leaves its mark upon the climber. I gazed into the cross-hatchings of a small hold, into the geometrical organization of crystals. The crack brought to me its unusual grain, shadow, illusion.

The earth was rotating, and thought sailed freely in my mind like clouds in the sky. There would never be another Don Whillans. I laughed and banged on. The hail left. The sky became blue and opened outward to infinity, toward the sun's corona. There were no more shadows. Climbing was a peculiar thing to do. But I was thankful to be drawn to it. A jewel fish in a beautiful domain.

The following short fiction story was published in the August 1986 issue of Rock 'N' Ice Magazine. I had just finished a university course in bio-psychology (study of the brain), and the disease of memory known as Korsakoff's syndrome — projected into the context of a climber — captured my imagination. My friend John Gill said about this story that I allowed myself about as much rope as would be required to hang myself.

Peril

In a mechanistic way, I stumbled into the life of old Joe Delacroix. Sitting beside each other on a bus, we were both physically energized by the movement of a lovely woman who sat down adjacent to us. Joe's eyes caught mine. His age was the life-affirming element of the situation.

Rapid progress could be made with Joe Delacroix. After a few sentences he and I were friends. He had been a mountaineer the best part of life and, discovering I was a climber, offered a spine-tingling account of a past adventure on rock. Joe placed his finger halfway down the page of a book he was holding and said, "According to Aristotle, the purpose of art is to capture the essential form of things." This made me laugh, because I thought at first he was still contemplating the young woman. I realized quickly that he actually loved art. He continued, "The purpose of art, according to Aristotle, is to depict the hidden meaning of things, the secret things beyond appearance."

I was soon to learn that his story was a tragic one. During the next month, seeing him several times again, he related experiences of his life — all but the last twenty years which were never mentioned. I acquired the details of his more recent life from his daughter Miro and his life-long best friend Mr. Georgez.

Joe had led a normal life as a young climber, except to drink excessively. Slowly his life had drifted into a dark impressionism. Joe began to develop a variety of Korsakoff's Syndrome, a disease of memory associated with chronic alcoholism. Victims of this disease can remember most of their earlier life. However, they do not remember new information for more than a few minutes. An individual with this disease can meet someone or read a newspaper, and a few minutes later fail to recognize the person or recall the newspaper. He will read it again. Each day starts afresh with memory only of early life. Joe was one of the very rare cases of Korsakoff's Syndrome who did not require being permanently institutionalized. I discovered that he was very easy to entertain with the same joke over and over again.

Yet Joe had never withdrawn the emotional investment in himself as a growing being with a future. When he was not able to visit the art galleries of the city, he carried his book of art. He studied the paintings of Rembrandt. He particularly liked El Greco's Christ. The immediate realism, although unremembered, did seem to leave some sort of impression upon his visual tastes. Art was the key in his struggles between hope and despair. He was self-crippled by alcoholism but intellectually very alive. His illness did not hinder his aesthetic contemplation. He showed a great ability to perceive art and had an inclination for feeling-reaction. Informed that he had an illness, he had forgotten ever being told. His previous life had instilled enough information about his environment that he would not forget which turns to make on the way home, or on the way to the mountains above his home, or to a gallery.

Although seventy years of age, Joe was by no means a worn out man. I suspected that his desire to climb had not died away either, rather that he might have simply intimidated all prospective partners. Mr. Georgez and Miro were intrigued by the idea that I would invite Joe on a moderately easy rock climb of minimal length. Joe seemed delighted by the invitation and was delighted again when I came to get him the morning of the climb. We gathered some carabiners, some gear, his rucksack with water and lunch, and a rope. He put his climbing shoes in the rucksack, and we started off. Just out the door, I returned to collect the rucksack because he had forgotten it. A short walk led us to the mountain behind his home. At one point he said we should turn right if we were going to the gallery. I told him we were going to climb. He was delighted.

At the base of the rock, I thought to test his memory. "Still use a bowline to tie in?" I asked. He took an end of the rope and answered my question. I was presumptuous. This was an excellent sign that his past climbing experience would unfold before his eyes. Perhaps I might even absorb something of this man's technique.

That he could see the rock, usually see me, feel the rope around his waist, and hear the light tap of his boot rubber against the holds would keep him constantly informed that he was in the midst of a climbing adventure. I remembered his comments about art. He had referred to "the essential form of things." For him, that could be only the moment, in its continual re-awakening. I reached a ledge a short distance up the rock and invited him to follow, in turn. As he climbed, I belayed the rope somewhat tight on him so he could re-experience climbing and feel secure doing so. As he moved upward toward me, I wondered what possible problems could occur as a result of his disease. Forgetting his age, would he assume he was capable of climbing faster than he should? By virtue of the clear sensory information of his surroundings, certainly there could be no chance he would forget altogether that he was climbing, suddenly unrope, and step into space as though out from a bus. Would he forget that his foot had been placed on a small hold? The result of this latter instance might be a harmless fall a few inches onto the rope. It would be important not to let him drowse off at a ledge, because there he would definitely forget, and it would prove, upon waking, a sudden jolt of acrophobia for him.

He did not seem inclined toward any of these problems and was elated. It did not bother me that he had no recollection of my name. Joe was at no loss for levities.

"Charming contrast to my usual soulless dissipation. We shall look forward to a night of debaucheries." The kindred spirit I felt from these words, from this man whose composure was keener than my own, transported me into his time when such pithy whispers thrown upward into a raspy breeze would have satiated all imagination. I was sad his current life suffered the interference of forgetfulness. He would forget we had climbed, and forget about debaucheries.

As I belayed him up to another ledge, he was glad to make my acquaintance and asked if he might join up with me for the remainder of the climb. I pointed out to him that we were already roped together.

"Swift work," he replied. By such ingenuousness, his lack of affectation, I was abased to the dust. I asked him what his best climb was. He could not remember. Nor, for that matter, could I remember mine. The body is a study in planned obsolescence, I thought. It wears out. But what a joy, I imagined, to be able to listen to hundreds of hours of conversation and be entirely immune to hatreds, falsehoods, or manipulations. Joe seemed devoid of strife, fear, love, and other stresses which afflict a normal human being. His was a quality of ready appeasement, with none of the nearest world horrors on tap. As he ascended, he was a composer. Indeed, he was yet a graceful climber.

As I began to drift idly upward, a short distance above him, suddenly a handhold broke loose. I found myself nearly falling. I managed to stay on the rock and not fall but was attached by only one hand. My feet had been thrust free by the violence of the occurrence. For the few seconds which followed, I was unable to get re-established on the rock and unable to find a new hold for my free hand. Falling appeared inevitable. A shoulder eased upward under my foot and gave to me its support.

I was astonished at how quickly Joe had recognized the situation, abandoned the security of the ledge, and moved up to me.

It was a very good day, I thought, when I stumbled in a mechanistic way into the life of old Joe Delacroix. Saving me was for Joe a castle in the sand, washed away with the next wave of experience. That he did not remember me or our climb was of little import. It would not negate the essential form of that day.

The following article, about climbing in England, is one of the most ambitious projects I ever attempted and may be, of all my writings, the most important to me. A professor at the University of Colorado, Reg Saner, encouraged me to submit the article to the English department's essay contest. I never did, because I wanted to keep working on it. A few sections of it were published in High Magazine, November 1984. Here is the article in its entirety.

"All in all, these pages combine the easy going advantages of the familiar essay, in all its whimsicality, and wry candor, with the scope of a panoramic survey. The eye of the narrator looks outward and inward, about and around. With the take-off of that narrator's homeward bound jet, momentum established by the essay's manifold English scenes and personal encounters moves toward a fulfilling close." —Reg Saner, Ph.D., winner of the Walt Whitman Award for Poetry and the National Poetry Series Open Competition

Faces Come Out Of The Rain

The raven, painted sinister by Poe
(did raven and the marlet ever meet?)
or dark by Shakespeare. Does the raven know
she is in literature a conceit?
I feel that I could stroke her feathered neck,
or perch with her on ledges, post on rocks,
and have her teach me as her young, let peck
me, somewhere throw me from a nest with squawks
to fly near her above a burdened plain,
a quiet, open path, go anywhere.
We weave through arcs of color, drunk on rain,
two carried up on lightly rising air.
But then we die and sail a final breath
as angels in the blackness of Macbeth.

People stare out from stone houses, across heather and through smoky, dark, hanging clouds between which, on the horizon, are openings into blue and light. In an afternoon, the rain has stopped. The air drips, newly clean. An ancient, Welsh mix of dim and bright distinguishes the scene, hills that circulate with fresh, wet fragrance and changes of light. There is the sound of a bird, or a child. To the west is the Irish Sea. Thirteen days spent in England in 1984 expressed for me perhaps more vividly than any other time of my life what I feel is mystical, important, and humanly fulfilling about the rock climbing experience. That short time, its web of adventures, the groomed green of the hills, nerve-stirring gritstone that I tried to ascend, and human events—how individuals touched one another—were, as I view them in retrospect, powerful and spiritual.

William Wordsworth held the conviction that the spiritual and the natural worlds were interrelated. He grew close to the English countryside, to its sky, and birds. He roamed the hills and knew the intrinsic strength that could be found in them. Among Wordsworth's statements of elemental emotions are found crags, thresholds, an idea that consciousness illuminates—but also contributes to—the organization of what one sees: "By earthly nature had the effect been wrought/ Upon the dark materials of the storm...."

The thought interested me that I might shape the rock just a little, as I climbed. As essential as climbing: was to think about it, and to write about it. Like writing, climbing makes you feel uneasy. You live with it in your thoughts, feel its process, how the logic struggles and corrects itself, an involvement with the folly, and the ethos, of the pictures.

Prior to my going to England, I had become very reflective about climbing. Although I was active in climbing, it was becoming more of an invisible study within the soul: less what you climbed than the love with which you knew the environment as you climbed, or as you walked, the proportion of feeling, observation, and appreciation that you gave to experience. There were times, for example, where it was possible to look at the physical world more openly, more acutely, or more honestly, where the rock, it seemed, acquired more beauty. I saw the elegance, the flow, and excitement of climbing movement as qualities that were found in nature. Contributing to these endeavors were, of course, friends, their own beauty, their multiple, almost folk, angles on the adventure.

A few non-climber friends wondered why I persisted so philosophically with climbing, and for as many years as I had, what climbing had brought to me really, if I would grow away from it ever. Climbing was now ingrained, as though where I was coming from was out of its weather, that who I was had to do with rock, with sky, or trees.

At first in climbing, if you accomplished something major, such as Yosemite's El Capitan, or if you created a free climb of an advanced grade, it was the tendency to assume that you were "there," an attitude germane to the younger, competitive spirit. After those kinds of years of intensity in my own climbing, I came to recognize that there were more transcendent propositions, involvements of a more lasting vein. The terrain itself, the natural aesthetics, had somehow assisted in the enduring quality of the experience slightly more than had any particular contrivance of difficulty on rock. With friends, you could have a laugh across experience. You could intuit your companion and stand inside each other's moves. Sharings of these types forme, for me, an enormous bank of reminiscence. I did take a measure of pride in my physical ability. Climbing from a purely athletic focus had its pleasures, almost a metaphysical satisfaction at times, and did not altogether bypass those "spiritual" objectives. There was the phenomena of staying power, the feeling of upward impetus, moments of mightiness, sorcery, the body led by the disclosures of kinesthesia.

I knew as well as any of the newest athletes the electricity, the barrage of possibilities, that climbing threw at a mind, and they were a magic that continued to affect me. Yet there was more, not expressed by difficulty gradings of climbs. Numbers, like money or time, were abstractions and less meaningfully communicated the idea of accomplishment. I thought of the insight of several of the best climbers of my day, Chuck Pratt, Royal Robbins, John Gill. I thought of an older friend, Baker Armstrong, who at age sixty soloed the thirteen hundred-foot Third Flatiron above Boulder, Colorado, in sixteen minutes. I had countless climbing friends who never had any recognition. But each had his or her personal kind of accomplishment. The mountains—their psychic, sonorous, spiritual realities—have a history as venerable as light. They are a dream where beauty wanders in its own way, and more interesting than the height that you think you should achieve is the individual strain of revelation into which you are drawn.

Most climbers have a sense of the mystical. Climbers in general, I believe, are informed, concerned with beauty, and have memorable interactions with people, yet at the same time are busy with their own vitality and can give the impression that reflection is not the highest priority. I have over-reacted at times to certain insensitivities and to an irrepressible segment of the climbing populace whose life work, it occasionally seems, is to hurry my role as a fading affiliate. Undoubtedly those who I imagine are the most earnest at this (who brandish biceps twice my size and gaze into gym mirrors) feel belittled when I sound off with doctrines of mystical awareness, something I do too often. I have not always had my own head turned to the right directions or climbed always with the appropriate degree of dignity, nor do I always now. So I have no place putting myself above anyone. In fact I am sympathetic toward young climbers and toward climbers in all their ages and varying approaches. My opinions exist because I have done a lot of thinking about climbing over the years. Climbing is important to me, and I have wanted to take it beyond burlesque. I speak of fortitude in the face of exhaustion, striving for an understanding that will motivate and nurture a slightly older, seasoned imagination.

I have stayed with climbing for what it gives my mind and soul and not for the small, steady financial benefits my reputation has allowed me to enjoy along the way. Article and book royalties, lectures, and teaching climbing have brought a modest income, but I am confident I would love climbing just the same if that income were gone or never existed. In the '60s I might have been statuesque enough to model climbing products, but I never did (I sometimes feel I model the gloom of the rock, an aura of fingers closing around a hold). For me the climber is more akin to the poet: to survive, most support themselves by a different means than poetry! Climbing is not grounded in these material measures by which society so often appraises a person. I never have had much money and appreciate a statement by William James that the squalid cash interpretation put on the word success is our national disease. There are finer illustrations embedded in rock's chapters that are an idea of the kind of life you know or person that you are. I have not objected too much to the times of financial despair. They are integrated in the life. I am a writer, artist, rock climber, almost as though unconsciously I relish the idea of professional disaster.

Outside my Boulder, Colorado, apartment, the air in the yard was cool, respirable. Afternoon. March light. Flowers, sun, clouds, mountains—their fragrances. This was one of those preservers of climbing, inspecting the casual particulars of nature. The literary term for the process: phenomenology. Much of my motivation was based in this interior profession, data emanating from the presented world and followed as though somewhere in it were a kind of "logic of fantasy." Phenomenology was the strength of much poetry, attempting to notice things, everything somehow a source of information or insight. Seemingly insignificant objects made a contribution, were necessary. A rock formation might contain a memory of other times or of a certain mood of life. The field of consciousness to which phenomenology was engaged reached also toward society, furniture, speech. It explored impulses of aggression, sex, or fear, how things deteriorated or were restored, the universal in the particular. No one could pretend to all of the nuances that constituted a given day or could recognize comprehensibly how forces of the universe cooperated. But something worthy of observation existed in most places. Darks, lights, contours, faces, opposition, contradiction, the attractively perturbing, the terrain of rock climbing. The yard of my house—in view of the mountains—had its trees, shrubs, little foliages, a green, wet smell of approaching spring. I felt a sense of commitment to these, a slight withdrawal into them, a feeling of having grown with them for a number of years, but a feeling also to do with origins, to do with my earliest memory of nature, how flowers and rock one day rose for me and became surprisingly a life.

Unexpectedly, I was given the opportunity of spending two weeks in England.

English climber-writer Jim Perrin liked a small book I had written, and he recommended me as a guest speaker for the National British Mountaineering Conference. An official letter of invitation came, along with round-trip plane fare. I had not been to England. The rock climbing photos of a book about Snowdonia had captured my imagination when I was in high school. England's elvish ruffian Don Whillans had climbed with me when he visited America in 1966, when I was in my late teens. He, Royal Robbins, and I did a couple of climbs in my home canyon, Eldorado. Before that encounter with Whillans, Royal wrote to me about adventures on British "gritstone," a coarse, excellent rock of which Whillans was a pioneer. In that letter, Royal spoke of Whillans' "fearful and brilliant" Sloth: a hand-sized crack leading out the underside of a large overhang. Whillans was the first to do the climb in the 1940's, in tennis shoes, setting a stone in a crack to run the rope behind for protection. From all descriptions, I imagined vile little men who smoked cigarettes, drank in pubs, and climbed to their limits on small, black, rain-lashed cliffs. Otherwise, my impressions of England were castles, tabards, and executioner blocks.

I once had received a letter from Tom Higgins who told how he fell off while trying to ascend a British sea cliff and dropped into the ocean. He fortunately only suffered a broken leg. It was not the type of occurrence, I supposed, that would ever come very near to me.

On receiving the invitation to the conference, and knowing that I would climb while I was in England, I found myself doing pullups on doorjambs. I had become rather provincial, enjoying a great deal of attachment to Boulder, Colorado. I did not look forward to the discomfort of rain. Gray Ringsby, a young climbing partner, was holding me in his initiative, and I did not want to break the momentum of those energies. I had not been to Europe and could only imagine the perils that would greet one there.

One night I watched an old episode of "The Twilight Zone" in which a plane flew from London to New York and went through a time barrier. Passengers looked down and saw dinosaurs! I was beginning to see things as omens.

I hated flying: committed to a tube of metal, lofted into the stratosphere, the claustrophobia. How would a flight feel of that length? Would I go crazy, run screaming down an aisle of the plane? Another night, I had a dream where I was lost in Britain, walking in a mixed-up city (which later proved to look very much like Manchester). In the dream, I wandered from door to door trying to find my way. I entered a house and made the queer discovery that its residents had photos of Eldorado climbing on their walls. For a day or two, I carried with me that dream's sense of the supernormal. Then I injured myself in two ways before leaving for Britain. I pulled a muscle in my forearm exercising on a rope ladder and broke a rib in karate practice. The injuries made it difficult to climb at all. Was I trying to create a way out? Or was I simply encountering the adversity that has seemed in my life to precede every experience of extreme worth?

I decided to face myself and led Supremacy Crack and Vertigo, two exacting free climbs in Eldorado Canyon. To some degree I was able to take my mind off the rib and arm. I wanted to climb in England. There would be time to recover from my injuries when I returned.

Before leaving, I happened to see several British films: Educating Rita, American Werewolf in London, and Chariots of Fire. Gray filled my head with David Bowie music. My friend John Gill gave me a "Baedeker" guide to Great Britain. Higgins wrote to me again of his trip to England, warning that I not fall in love — I would not be able to afford the transatlantic phone bill. My chess partner Eugene Salome refused to play chess with me on sunny days, wanting me to follow through in getting in shape on the rock. Betty and Baker Armstrong screened the climbing slides I would show at the festival, and Betty sewed a few of my clothes. Tom Frost gave me a watch. My parents mailed a travel bag to me, along with two hundred dollars. David Allan, shaking my hand, passed a hundred dollar bill to me. I had not asked anyone for anything. It amazed me the way so many were caught up in my going to England. I felt as though I would be a representative for them all.

My father wisecracked, "You can't go to Britain. You don't speak British." David Hart, a professor friend, suggested that I speak slowly and afix "o"s to my words (I am Ameri...can...o). The fact of the matter was that I would struggle at times in England to communicate. For example, when British climber Dennis Gray inquired, "Are you into training?" I thought he asked, "Are you entertaining?" I told him that I was.

It occurred to me that I might invite someone to go on this adventure with me. Since Gray was in school, I asked Charlie Fowler who was a relatively new friend and an excellent climber. We'd done a few climbs together, but I didn't really know him. He seemed to lack conversational ability or simply was quiet. I had always needed to draw him out. Perhaps in England we would melt the taciturnities.

During the long, toilsome flight eastward, a moon shone on the jet wing and below us illuminated clouds which covered the ocean. I didn't sleep. We arrived at Heathrow Airport at sunrise, the plane coming down from blue sky into a thick layer of clouds that covered London. Customs asked who I was. I said a climber, they said, "Pass on." Charlie and I met a crowd of people holding signs with names written on them. One sign read, "Pat Ament, the BMC." Artist-climber Roger Durban was our escort through the crowded streets of London. He drove wildly toward a train depot, never ceasing to deliver friendly chat. We stopped long enough to see Westminster Abbey, Parliament, the Thames. Bobbies strolled along the sidewalk in stern, well-postured ways, gunless. I had Charlie take my picture alongside one of them, at which point I felt they sized me up as a stupid tourist. Roger informed us that Bobbies were no longer called Bobbies and were now the "fuzz." I changed a few dollars into pounds, my first purchase a bagel, postcards, and hot chocolate. As change I received a lot of coins the worth of which I did not try to suppose, diplomatically dropping them into a pocket and thanking the proprietor. Larger than American coins, the equivalent of five dollars bulged my jingling pockets.

Taxis — black, shined, frenzied. Red double-decker buses driving in the left lane. A few people rode horses, others bikes. Sixteen pounds bought a second-class, wood bench on a train. It was a train electrically powered, blue-greenish cars. England sailed by the window — hills green, houses made of stone, mist, wooded fields, werewolves, ghosts, knights of the middle ages, England, a medieval land, fog, sorcerers, smoke, industry, art, social classes obstinate with heritage. Chronic drinkers of tea, beer. People happy, tender, heartless, hideous, spiritual apathy or revival, people out of work, disillusionment with government, the game of cricket. Urban sights, sounds, psychopaths, suicides, yet also qualities opposite of deranged — the quiet, the pastoral, the idyllic.

Bob Dylan came to mind, his concert tour of Britain and the film "Don't Look Back." I heard his harsh harmonica, saw Dylan as he studied England quietly through the window of a moving train.

Charlie and I were greeted in Manchester by an exuberant, young Ian Dunn, yellow hair streaming down to his shoulders. He was the first of many who were appointed to receive us at places along the journey. He drove us to BMC headquarters to meet the president of the BMC, Dennis Gray. Ian was ready to show us every climb in Britain and would have, given time. Under the strain of the travel I was slightly insolent, oblivious to my jet-blown hair and unwashed train face. Jet lag had taken a toll, and I began to sense that my irritableness was putting Ian off. Charlie and I decided to explore the streets of Manchester by foot and quickly discovered a climbing shop. I looked through a book of climbing photos of France's Patrick Edlinger. At this time there were no English climbing shops that had the new Patrick Edlinger climbing shoe. I had seen it in Colorado and now wanted to buy a pair, but no luck. Charlie, bored, returned to BMC headquarters. I sat in a small restaurant and ate a fish 'n' chips. Suddenly I had a chilling thought that I was lost — as in my dream.

In Britain, French fries were "chips," potato chips "crisps." Cookies were "bisquits." To line up was to "queue up." Women were "birds." The drugstore was "the Chemist's." To go away was to "piss off." The word "piss," while being a vulgarism in America, had several common and acceptable uses in British. For example, Ian MacNaught Davis: "Love to take the piss out of Jill Lawrence." She was one of Britain's foremost female climbers, he a little heavy and out of shape but a master of the barbed response. Ken Wilson, during a climb he and I did in Staffordshire, said to a complete stranger passing underneath us, "Can you take some photos of us with our camera, or are you going to piss off?" Parking lots were "car parks," cigarettes "faggots." Ken reminded me that English was the parent language to American. One person said that my problem was that I read Webster's Dictionary.

Breezes whistled through houses, and most houses were as cold as outside. Houses were centuries old, no central heating. Brits used tea or coffee ("brews") as another kind of central heating. The herb tea syndrome gave me problems in the middle of the night. Sleeping in full clothing, with coat and hat (bivouac style), buried deep in clothes and under covers, finally shivering to sleep, I would then feel the need to visit the "water closet." Bathrooms were an interesting study in England. They had tubs but rarely showers. I preferred a shower. I did not like to bathe in my own dirt. Usually wash basins were separated from the "toilet," and so to wash your hands you had to move to a room elsewhere — trying not to touch anything along the way. Faucets were divided — hot boiling out of one side, freezing out of the other. This division presented challenges, for example when attempting to rinse your mouth.

I provoked waitresses by ordering foods out of their proper sequence. It was wrong to order a fish 'n' chips and then a side of beans. It put waitresses in a quandary that I would order water. In a country where weight was measured in "stones" and money in "pounds," where a question such as "How far to Oxted" was answered with "Five stops," I was indeed a foreigner and England a foreign land.

The first night, in Manchester, Ian took us to an indoor, artificial climbing wall, one of countless which enliven British sport-athletic "halls." The wall flowed with climbers, twenty or thirty moving up, down, across, the handholds of one serving as the footholds of another. Ian traversed soundly over favorite moves. His blond hair blew in the stale, chalky air. His wife Claudi, petite, French, climbed strongly. Ian told how in the afternoon he had been to a climbing shop where an employee said, "Tell Mr. Ament that I could grasp the holds but not the problem." It was a quote from my book Master of Rock and instilled in me a deep sense of welcome. Attempting to traverse the climbing wall, both my rib and forearm hurt. I stepped back to the floor and expressed to Ian that I was injured and had better save what I had for the actual climbing on rock. The euphoria was shattered suddenly by Charlie who blurted, "Quit making excuses, Pat. You don't have to make excuses." The room hushed, climbers in suspension between holds, a moment so fierce that I turned away. The climbing soon resumed, but a tone had been set for Charlie and me. I registered my disapproval of his remarks, but he was undissuaded. I probably did make too many excuses, but these people didn't know it yet. At least I could be allowed those excuses that were legitimate.

After the wall, Ian fattened us on dinner at an Indian restaurant. Then, fully clothed, I crawled into my sleeping bag atop a bed in Ian's apartment. In the morning he drove us to a gritstone climbing area called The Roaches, the location of Whillans' intimidating overhang known as The Sloth. We drove along a beautiful, green hill above a lake. This was Staffordshire—hills, grass, brown heather, sheep. Along a severely narrow road through a village, we passed a brick house with a sign that read "Beware, overhanging roof"—an interesting foreshadow. A hike led past a sinister, stone house that was the residence of a hermit. We passed a door which had written on it, "No trespassing or I'll shoot U." Ian assured us that the hermit hadn't chased anyone with an axe for some time and was probably not at home. Smoke flowed from the chimney of the house. We carefully moved upward through green, mossy forest, up a kind of staircase naturally formed of stone above the house, to The Roaches and to the safety of an overhanging roof.

I wanted to lead The Sloth. Charlie offered no resistance. I was wary of him, but he suddenly said to Ian, "Pat's a master of crack climbing." One minute I had been an excuse maker, the next a master climber. I pondered these sounds. But the tensions lessened, and I led upward toward that old '40s roof. A fine rain emitting a gentle, mistlike light drizzled down around the edges of the rock. The roof required that I climb horizontally outward, my legs hanging ostentatiously free at one instant, hands wedged in the crack of the roof.

I reached a trapeze-sized hold and waited, as though to prolong the route. In the '40s, the route was a fantastic whimsy. Drops of rain slowly seemed to pick the places they would settle on rock. Striations seemed composed on the rock by wind. I heard the noise of shoes when they would press against the grain of the rock. The area was ghostly, beautiful, mythological, a route with themes of temptation and redemption. The acoustics of the area allowed for a clarity of sound that was phenomenal. Where my hand was between holds, it dipped into my chalk bag. Chalk was smudged on my pants near my hip. Charlie scrutinized me, to make certain that my demeanor was professional, that I did not mismanage a move. Climbing together these few days would practice his patience. I could ritualize fascination, waiting, looking, getting to know a route's requirements before I met them, moves with themes of doomed youth and beauty, moves of dark fatalism and stark, poetic fire.

Samuel Johnson was twice jailed for debt. A haphazard thought.

I tried not to make a production out of the route. I assessed it immediately as within my ability. Cracks suited my constitution, cracks where hands could wedge inside. I felt an affinity for the position under the overhang, how I could look straight down to Charlie standing below. He held the rope somewhat inattentively. The overhang looked more precarious than it was, allowing me to feel that I was a more exciting climber than I was. Doing this route was my only concern of the day. I stretched backward, outward, upward. I imagined how this place was at night, its moonlight, its emotion, clouds whitening as they passed across the moon's light. Was the hermit in his house? Did he go for walks during the night?

There were climbs of such extreme that to do them you had to become pathologically violent yet possess micro-skill. At times in the past, when I was fit, when I had endless energy to train, I had attained such levels. But in large part I had drifted away to chess, piano, line drawing, filmmaking, study of poetry, and writing. Climbing remained there, but I could choose the days I wanted it. I was capable of being weak-willed, flabby, groggy. Not long ago, a love affair followed by a bout with Bailey's Irishcreme had left me twenty pounds heavier. I found I had to abort boulder routes I could once do in penny-loafers. Meanwhile climbers mis-equated exertion with virility or strength with sharpness of thought. A part of me took exception now to strength climbing, likely because it seemed unfair how short my day in the sun—strengthwise—was. I was finding another type of strength in karate. In climbing, there was pleasure in ticklish technique to solve strength moves. With the Herculean bodies of today's climbers, technique was an old has-been's last salvation. Ian scrambled up an easy edge of the rock to get some photos from the side as my feet, legs, and body swung free into space. One of the key holds felt thin, ready to break off. The chalk on my hands and moisture of the air became a paste. The route held all of the reason for one of Whillans' stoic, cutting rejoinders.

After completing the climb, we found a fifty-foot, steep wall that Ian said we should each solo. He insisted we do so and went up first to set the example, at one point leaping dynamically for a hold. I didn't like the idea of climbing unfamiliar rock without a rope. Ian insisted that I would be all right and that Dennis Gray, the president of the BMC, had forbidden him to kill me before the conference. Afterwards would be O.K., but not before. On that note we soloed. The last one to achieve the final hold, I caught sight of someone watching from a ridge of rock above and to my left. The person was standing against mist, silhouetted in sky, almost camouflaged in it. He stared at me. I glanced away from him, then looked again, and he was gone. Was it the recluse? I did not tell Charlie or Ian what I saw and chose to believe that in that glance the person and I had struck some understanding. Ian, Charlie, and I were satisfied for the day and descended through mist and heather.

Later that evening, Dennis, the president of the British Mountaineering Club, took charge of us and drove us to his house fifty miles north of Manchester, near the University of Leeds—where we were rushed to an engagement with a second indoor climbing wall. Dennis held us in his spell with stories of Whillans and Joe Brown, tales of wild, drunken, stormy, British climbs. Dennis owned a climbing shop set at one end of his home. The door of the shop opened to a street busy with cars and various shops. The living side of the house was quiet, and its door opened to a peaceful residential street. I took a bath and soaked in my dirt. I was given a room to sleep in—no bed, but a good floor. There was an upright piano I played in the morning in a large, pink, silly hat my mother had knitted. Dennis began to prepare breakfast, as Charlie and I waited at a large table made of wood. Dennis' wife entered the kitchen and scolded him for trying to use some bacon that was weeks old. He gave the dog the bacon. Dennis complained of sore gums and with a finger rubbed clove on them.

We drove eastward for an hour to Buxton, where the national conference was to be held. Charlie and I were given a large room in the Old Hall Hotel, an elegant, ancient building where Mary Queen of Scots had found "first-class stabling." The hotel was across the street from the opera house and pavillion gardens where the festival would take place. People scurried about, looking for pubs, or sitting at tables in groups, arguing, drinking tea and rich, dark "pints" dripping over their edges. I snapped photos, outside admired medieval architecture—old, brown stone buildings in mist. There was a large area of grass with stream and ponds. Mansions, trees, air blowing. Birds chittered. At this moment a man in a suit walked by, perhaps in his late fifties, lean, with white hair. His skin was brown, possessing a radiance. His tender, dignified eyes greeted mine. He was Italian. I recognized him as one of the other guest speakers, Walter Bonatti—perhaps the most famous alpinist of all time. He shook my hand. Through his translator, Mirella Tenderini, we introduced ourselves. She greeted me warmly, said one of her missions was to get an interview with me for an Italian climbing magazine. She said that Walter was aware of my name. People began to photograph him and me together. It seemed slightly affected, since we had barely met, although something instantaneous did exist—mutual and acknowledged by both Walter and me. We parted, away to organize ourselves in the hotel. Later, in a quiet, simple, carpeted room of the hotel, a room with only a few chairs and a piano, Walter and I met again. I kneeled on the carpet near his chair. Mirella translated. Charlie sat with us, on occasion shared a thought. Mirella was visionary, seeing inside us, bringing to Walter my mind and to me the amicability of Bonatti. After a time, she explained that he was conscious of an unusualness, a sensitivity, in me. He spoke of our closeness, of our spiritual rapport, a feeling of harmony between us despite out different climbing styles. I was solely a rock climber, he a mountaineer. The discourse was occasionally brightened by the flash of a camera from someone nearby. Dennis passed, offered a short ridicule of me in Churchillian rhetoric.

Near the end of two and a half or three short hours, Mirella wished she'd had her tape recorder on. Walter offered the insight that if she'd had the tape recorder running there wouldn't have been anything of value said. Walter stated that he found in me some contradictions, but that they were pleasing ones. He was a man of unusual experience. I told him how I had, at the age of fourteen, written to the famous German climber Toni Hiebler, that I'd acquired a book of German, replaced my English words with German counterparts, and made a letter. Hiebler wrote back, requesting that I write in English—it was easier to understand. Walter laughed. Mirella disappeared to fetch her small cassette recorder. While she was gone I played the piano for Bonatti. It was a short piece, soft, melodic, created improvisationally as though it reflected upon what had been spoken. Music was a language that did not need translation. Mirella returned. Chris Bonington arrived at this time, one of Britain's fabled mountaineers. Historically, Bonatti and Bonington had had a painful disagreement concerning some climb. Now as they met, it was time for that to be gone. Enough years had passed. Their handshake turned the amber light to steel.

People raced off to a disco where Whillans was expected. Walter, Mirella, and I were worn out and decided to retire to our separate rooms. My lecture would come soon, with morning. I would be the first speaker, Walter the last. I thought through my presentation, sorted slides, contemplated the fact that Bonatti, perhaps Whillans, and a thousand people or more would be there to listen, to watch. I decided that I would wear the new, dark blue, Helly-Hansen jacket Dennis let me purchase at his climbing shop for half price. Past midnight I was still awake, long after Charlie had returned from discoing. He snored in a bed on the other side of the room.

I was up early, walking with slide trays through rain. I crossed the street, eager to get set up, and waited behind an aged gentleman with a cane who was trying to walk through the pavillion door with his umbrella open. He was, as Yeats described, a "tattered coat upon a stick" and took a step forward, but the umbrella above his head was wider than the door. He stepped back, frustrated, then tried again. He called loudly for his wife: "Isabelle!" Unexpectedly he turned to me and stared into my eyes. He was a few inches from my face. "Whaarrr's my wyfe!!!?" Caught off guard, I glanced in all directions for his wife, walked out to the street to see if I might locate her. She appeared from inside the pavillion, gently turned him around, and led him away. He muttered a complaint as his short steps gathered speed along the incline of the walk. I wondered if he had been a mountaineer.

I stood alone a few moments on the opera house stage, gazed at seats that would soon be filled. I felt alone, and separate from people in general. First to enter was Jill Lawrence, one of Britain's most respected climbers. We had climbed together the year before in Yosemite. She stepped onto the stage and gave me a hug. She was beautiful, I thought, a kind of liberated woman with curly dark hair and funny glasses. I gazed upward into the dim, multi-tiered depth of the opera hall.

I went backstage to be alone with my thoughts. A thousand people entered the hall. The person who introduced me to the audience said my talk would be called "American Heroes" and that it was "largely autobiographical." This brought a good laugh from everyone. There was almost deafening applause when I walked onto the stage. At first a little scared, I was in my element here— performer, oddball, in front of an audience of doctors, lords, ladies, counts, fox hunters, "layabouts," deadbeats, coal miners, iconoclastic climbers, scholars, classes, British humor sitting in endless rows and three levels, balconies above and to either side. People stood along the walls. I was the lonely center of attention. They were pleased that I could take the piss out of myself. I traced the history of my climbing, tales of Kor, Robbins, Pratt, Higgins, Gill, Breashears, Gray, their Whillans.... I had a slide of Whillans from when he and Royal and I climbed in Eldorado in 1966. Friendship persisted as my theme. Slides dissolved into one another, accompanied on occasion by a tape of some musical selection. Near the end of the talk, during slides of the exposed, final headwall of El Capitan, was a song by Arlo Guthrie:

> "Lonely sunshine, days come easy,
> many friends, they come and go,
> know there's a lot of feeling
> that I've left behind...
> like a sailor sailing over Jordan
> on the road back home again...
> Oh were I the last to leave,
> would these ribbon highway roads
> be less wonderful to me?
> Why must I always be so slow?"

These lyrics hit home for me more so than they had before and would from this time be deeply associated with England. As the song played I thought how blessed I had been as a climber, how much meaning climbing held for me in the years I had done it, and that England was the fruition of my climbing experience, or at least an inspired endpiece, being with Bonatti.... The final slide was of a freight train, the method by which I had gotten back home to Colorado from Yosemite after climbing El Capitan, the young hobo climber's passage in golden days.

Backstage in a dressing room, as I put slides away, I glanced up into a mirror that had colored light bulbs around its edges and saw, standing behind me, a short bearded man. It was Don Whillans, hard man, author of Sloth, comic, brilliant, in whose presence even the strongest company tended to become servile, a climber who happened at a time in Britain when climbing needed an imaginative touch. The eighteen years since I had seen him in Eldorado had not changed him, the spirit perceptible within the tattered, weathered, rounding, North Wales shell. He confessed that he had slipped out of my lecture for a minute to fetch a beer at the bar and, as he was told, missed the part about himself. He offered to buy me a beer. Not a drinker, I was talked into trying a "shandy" (lemonade spiked with beer). Climbers gathered. With compliments, a few tried to insinuate themselves into Whillans' good graces. He growled slightly. Cameras clicked. Whillans listened as two young climbers debated the virtues of mental ability versus physical strength. Whillans offered the conversation crusher, "Wha eef yooou don't 'ave either?"

I told him that he looked good, and he replied, "I'm sti' alive," and, pointing to the sky, "They dooon't want me oop there." He mused, "I'll gooo down there," pointing to the floor. He was speaking over the world's heads. About a year and a half later he would die mysteriously in his sleep. I would need to learn of his death to realize the full blessing of seeing him now again.

A woman arrived, looking very enterprising, who said that there was a present for me. Promising Whillans that I would return soon, I excused myself and left him to enjoy the infirmities of the hour. My gift: a pair of Patrick Edlinger shoes, no one knew from whom. Their new smell took me back to how climbing had fed my soul when I was a boy, the wind in trees, smell of pine, the tinkle of pitons in a small pack as I hiked upward in anticipation. On the way back to Whillans, I was intercepted by Jill Lawrence, then met one of the younger English climbing stars, Ron Fawcett. Someone next directed me to Jim Perrin. It was Jim who had recommended me as guest speaker. He sat at a table in the pavillion, wore something like a suit without a tie. He had long, rough hair, dark brown. He wore glasses. He had one glass eye. We had not yet met except for a short phone conversation when I arrived in

Don Whillans, Buxton, England, Spring of 1984. Photo by Pat Ament.

Manchester, where I phoned him at his home in Wales. During that phone conversation, he invited me to his home and placed in my thoughts images of Welsh rock climbs that were not far from where he lived. Jim sat at the table mysteriously, and the meeting seemed odd, slightly cold, perplexing in that, as I learned, the man most responsible for my trip to England had failed to be at my talk. He'd slept in, he said. Nevertheless, we confirmed that we would climb in a day or two in Wales.

Returning to Whillans, I said, "I had to get these shoes." He said, "Thooot maybe you took them to be re-sooouled." Whillans, Ian MacNaught Davis, and I moved across the street to a little pub in the hotel. They drank, told stories. Whillans spoke of his recent scuba diving exploits, how easy it was to do a one-finger pullup under water. He told of purchasing a new car, driving it into the sand on the beach, getting stuck, and watching the tide slowly take the car away, not to be seen again. He prided himself in his misconduct. Glancing at the program for the festival, Whillans donned a pair of octagonal bifocals which sat low on his nose. Later he was an acute observer of himself, during the conference as a member of a panel discussion in lively Brit style. His answers brought tumultuous laughter. "Don, how do you feel about climbing versus marriage, it's said they don't mix." Don: "Is that a twwooo-pawt question?" Later in the conference he participated in a fashion show where several climbers, including Dennis, demonstrating their grace and agility, sashayed onto the stage dressed as women. When Whillans bowed to the audience, he raised the back of his dress to the all-female group of judges at a table behind him. We wondered if he had any underwear. He was crowned beauty queen and set upon a throne (a chair), hailed by the masses, drunk, topped by a crown made of pointed papers pasted to a climber's helmet. I recalled climbing with him in Eldorado eighteen years earlier, his leading boldly above Royal and me, the rope hanging freely down the wall.

The Buxton festival closed with Bonatti. Before going on stage, he shook my hand—he said for luck. Mirella sat by his side on stage, to translate. Accompanying his talk with a few slides, he communicated his climber's life. It was a life that was rich but also painful. He had been criticized by the press for surviving a climbing disaster in which a couple of his companions died. Then were photos of great solo climbs of a more aloof Bonatti as he found his way alone through difficult, self-imposed challenges in the mountains and who for many years shunned the public. Bonington, sitting next to me in the audience, whispered to me, "He's simply a star." I admired Bonatti's ability for thinking, understanding, and the speed of his ideas—given sharply but with sensitivity. At one moment Mirella had difficulty in holding back a tear. It was a struggle to choke back one or two of my own. At the end, backstage in darkness, Bonatti embraced me and then, speaking for the first time in English, made the observation, "You and I are alpha and omega." By a single phrase, one could sense the strength of a person's understanding. The comment suggested our difference in age and our contrasting approaches to climbing, and that I was the first speaker and he the last. Part of the sentence's payload was delivered later by Mirella: "In the circle of life, alpha and omega meet." I remembered, with guilt, how as a youth I tore a photo of Bonatti out of a library book and pasted it into my private scrapbook of climbing. We had another conversation in the evening in the hotel, by the piano, then joined other climbers in the supper hall of the hotel. I chatted with Yugoslavian Alex Kunaver and a humble man over fifty who I learned was Eric Jones—he had recently soloed The Eiger. Dennis Gray and Bonington were there. Mirella took photos of all.

In the morning, I got up and wrote a small poem for Bonatti and gave it to Mirella to either translate or, if it wasn't any good, throw away. Bonatti autographed some postcards for me and wrote on one for a friend of mine, Dorene Frost, who was studying Italian. Mirella confided in me what Walter wrote on that card. He had found me to be "a wonderful ambassador of friendship."

Walter brought Charlie, Mirella, and me to his room for a final brief chat which Mirella taped. I said that if I could ever climb on those sunny Italian spires of the Grigna, where Walter had done his first climbs, I would feel that my climbing was complete. Charlie snickered, asking me if I wasn't getting a little schmaltzy. Bonatti said we would meet one day in Italy and climb. It would be three years before I would come to Italy and climb in the Grigna, but Bonatti would be on an expedition somewhere else at the time. In the street between the hotel and deserted opera house, as Bonatti prepared now to leave for Italy, he took me aside, embraced me again, gazed into my eyes, and whispered slowly, articulately, "Ciao, Pat," words with a tone that contained a meaning for me alone. He moved out into the street, turned, and stood for an instant, waved to me, and then, smiling and waving out the window of a car, vanished down a street.

Mirella stayed behind in England to finish her journalistic tasks, to interview me, for example, which she did that day in the room of the hotel, in the carpeted room with the chairs and the piano. I rattled off some marginalia about climbing, with her tape recorder running, but my thoughts were like the room—somewhat indefinite, lacking Bonatti's presence. I thought that this lady had, on a stage the night before, been also a star.

Ken Wilson, English climber and first editor of Mountain Magazine, drove Mirella, Charlie, and me to a gritstone cliff of Yorkshire called Stanage. Mirella came along with us to take a few pictures. Rain lightly accompanied us. There was a breeze. Ken was exuberant, loud. What with the cold, he demanded that we solo climb and that we each find our own route. He argued that it was too cold for anyone to stand in one place and belay. Was I to be manipulated into soloing again? The conference was over, and they no longer needed to keep me alive.

To climb in my coat was cumbersome. I scrambled up a large block of steep but moderate rock, in more or less a spirit of play, trying to warm up, enjoying the rock and open view of luxuriant, green terrain with its lakes and occasional country house. Mirella took her photos of us all. Ken and Charlie scampered up a short, easy route. I had noticed a thin, vertical crack piercing a wall and now studied it, certain it was what I should climb. I carried a rope and equipment to its base. Ken shouted from a distance, "The belayer's fingers will freeze. Soloing is the order of the day! Come on, man, solo solo solo!" I uncoiled the rope, sat defiantly at the bottom, and quietly psychoanalyzed myself. Racing down from a

Walter Bonatti and Pat Ament, Buxton, England, Spring of 1984. Photo by Mirella Tenderini.

second solo, Ken lumbered back, "O.K., man, I'll belay you, I'll suffer for you." Somehow his ravings did not offend me. They were all-inclusive, directed to me and to anyone. With my refined, personalized system of equipment—slider nuts, small "friends" (camming devices), skyhooks, bungee cords for opposition, tiny R.P. nuts, hip belay instead of belay plate, swami belt instead of seat harness, pink knitted hat instead of helmet, Patrick Edlinger shoes, and double rope—Ken went wild, finding new sources to disturb and to fascinate him. "I can see I'm going to have to teach you how to do these things right!" he said, adding, "You Americans are such technical idiots. Typical American reactionary behavior." And so forth.

I led up the finger crack, employing very little of my equipment and feeling relaxed without it but liking that I had it in case it was needed. The crack faded away, and I found friction with the palms of my hands on sloping holds. The edges of my shoes seemed to go to the right places. Ken expressed approval of my performance, saying, "You're building up some points on this one. Well done." I belayed from above, and he struggled a bit on the crack. A young woman by the name of Geraldine happened along and climbed the crack with us, then showed me a seventy-foot wall. Ken, unhappy with the thought that I was safe, stood near: "Solo that! Solo solo solo!" Suddenly I was forty feet above the ground, ropeless, in my coat and hat, rain soaking sharp, tiny holds. My fingers hurt from the cold, then I couldn't feel them, as though there were no flesh and I was supported by my fingerbones alone. I happened to notice Ken below watching. He sensed my uncertainty and said with a sardonic smile, "Well I guess you've go' a bit uv a problem then don't you?" As the climbing warmed my body, the numbness of my fingers wore off. My fingers stung now.

Geraldine sympathized with me. "Right, then," she said, assuring me that the climb was only "5-c" (the American equivalent of 5.9+ or 5.10-, difficult enough). I proceeded upward, thinking sarcastically that it was better to do something dangerous than to give up my bold front. This surrealism was being played in a tender, mist-invaded light. I was still partly asleep from jet lag. As I climbed, I thought of England's social medicine. I thought of the prince, his fox hunts, how they would cut the fox's feet before the chase to ensure the prince's success. In my mind were faces of road workers I had seen one morning who were pausing for a smoke and tea. I reached the top and then descended an easy route, ready for more lethal encouragements. The rain was intermittent, and we bouldered along the base of Stanage. I devised a short boulder problem. Charlie fell off it, five feet to the ground, and said, "These shoes are really slippery when they're wet." I retorted, "Stop making excuses."

Ken drove all of us to a uniquely British habitat, the "climber's cafe," a place which sells both brew and climbing gear. There were climbing photos above the tables. Here Ken gave Charlie and me to Jim Perrin who was at the cafe. That afternoon, in rain, Jim drove us toward Wales. I did not get to see most of the drive, unfortunately falling asleep in the back seat. I did wake up the last part of the drive, through Llanberis Pass, where Jim pointed out the striking rock formation of Cenotaph Corner. High on a hill, the impressive, symmetrical inside corner looked cold, bleak, its gray rock dripping, fresh with rain. A legendary accomplishment of Joe Brown, it was one of the climbs I most wanted to try. It looked more formidable, more ominous, than any historical photo had been able to convey.

It was late afternoon. We stopped at a boulder by the road where Jim pulled up on some holds and threw his heel onto a ledge above his head. We breathed the air, touched the rock, and returned to the car. Jim dropped us off at the house of Brede Arkless. Her house sat high in heather, near the foot of the inland mountains of Snowdonia and overlooking the Irish Sea. It was a small, two-story, white stone house alone from other neighboring houses. Sheep grazed nearby. Roads and property were bordered by two-foot high rock walls built by hand. These little walls extended for miles in all directions. A few rays of sun came through the clouds and fell beautifully around the house. Bleak Welsh cold blew outside as well as through the house. Rain began. The two eldest of Brede's eight children prepared a meal for us, breads, meat, spread out elegantly on a huge, wooden table that was linened. They filled us with warm fluids. I had "Barley Cup," a blend of roasted barley, rye, and chicory in boiling water. I liked the cozy domesticity of the children and found a place close to them by the fire. Our mother, Brede—a climbing guide by profession—was away training on an indoor climbing wall.

The genealogy on my Irish side leads to England and eventually to one Anthony Tipton who, as a youth in the Royal Army, was knighted during the campaign of Edward I to defeat Llewelyn, Prince of Wales in 1282. The Welsh were defeated at the battle of Snowdon Mountain, right here where I was. Llewelyn fled the battle on horseback, pursued by Tipton. As both were crossing Bulith bridge, an engagement took place in which Llewelyn fell mortally wounded. Tipton held an all night vigil, and the King arrived the following day. When it was determined that the slain man was indeed the Prince of Wales, Anthony was knighted on the field.

Time was passing. It was near end of March, 1984, evening holding a last color that seemed urgent and magnificent. While climbers were hustling-up their senses of personal importance, life was passing with such fineness, spiritually, with such an impression of smallness in eternity, that either one did not feel at all or life hit home hard—as in seeing the color of an evening.

I started rock climbing in 1958 or '59, as a seventh grader. I noticed the flatiron rocks above Boulder, Colorado, and began to explore in the hills around them. There was a spirit that was subtle, powerful, and very still. Quickly a series of acquaintances made me a member of Boulder's small rock climbing community. Through the years there was a continual, changing, apocryphal biography of me. Because I was excited, insecure, impressionable, in some ways impetuous, insipid, alienable, and high-flown, because I was too immersed to grow up and because the anarchism of my adolescence extended beyond all anticipated ends, because I had no sense of tribal boundaries, because I most definitely was a unique and curious — however unsophisticated — creature, I was liked by some and evoked the disdain of others. Also there were circles in which a person good at something was an irritant. I had an intensity, as well as naivety, and my success as a climber at a young age created suspicion, if not jealousy, in segments of the community. Some of my tormentors were aggravated by references to me which appeared in local papers, for example the Estes Park Trail: "Pat Ament, formidable area rock wizard." There were people who, as a defense, affected superior intellect and others who dismissed me as egotistical. They flattered themselves into thinking they knew what was really going on. Egotism is more often than not a sense of loneliness accompanied by a lack of self-esteem. The person compensates for his aloneness by giving himself recognition and attention, often a subconscious process that people mistake for self-love. Self-love is a different problem where a person is so infatuated with himself that he is unable to care about other people. My love for other people was the foundation of my writing, if not my whole existence. Yet I had that need for acceptance. Sometimes I would win over a detractor by the persistent frivolity with which I accepted myself into his company, violating his pleas for seclusion. There were individuals who saw fit to teach and endure with me and by whose example my actions increased in integrity. I was an archetype of the heroes by whom I was enthralled: Robbins, Gill... I started to wear a somber, almost angry shell. I could be gregarious and genial and remained caring — but among people who earned my trust. You could be surprised to learn, through the grapevine, that you were a number of things better or worse than you even knew. The search for self made me self-conscious, and the desire to share whatever was original in me brought foolishness and failure. Out of a kind of wicked sense of fun, I tried sometimes to be worthy of the somewhat covert hatreds of the least concilliatory of peers. By opening my mouth thoughtlessly, I also sometimes damaged relationships I had with friends. Yet there were the effects of light, the sunshine in trees, or on surfaces of rock, the lucidity of a tiny climb, sky to which you were attuned, a detached, perplexed amusement about whatever you had failed or succeeded at so far. Although divided by the signals I generated in others, I tried to realize the power of these years. A walk in the mountains, or climbing, invariably brought an intelligibility to life where otherwise there was turmoil. I was proud of climbing and of what I was able to have published, in the '60s and '70s an unpolished but improving writer.

At the outset of my climbing, in 1959, I had all the makings of valor except courage. Attracted to gymnastics, I excelled at coordination and balance. I trained obsessively at gymnastics for several years and worked out on the hardest climbing I could find—of a slightly higher standard than what was found near Boulder at the time. I consumed the big wall routes that held any mystique for me, such as El Capitan, Sentinel West Face, the Diamond, and was able to pioneer gymnastic tests on boulders. I eliminated the use of direct aid on a few sparkling, two and three-pitch routes around Boulder, Colorado, and in Yosemite. I was lean, my hands strong. I learned a slow, hollow-back press into a handstand, starting from a straight-body position lying face down on the floor. I mastered a slow muscle-up on a bar: starting from a hang, pulling to the chin-up position, and continuing slowly higher, without bringing one elbow up before the other, ending above the bar, supported by my arms. This did not make me "bold," in terms of climbing without protection. I wasn't as automatic as Kor, as brilliant or pure as Robbins, Pratt, or Higgins, as strong as Gill, nor a prodigy such as Breashears, yet I had something that was my own. Always I continued to go through phases of insecurity with acquaintances who questioned me as I questioned myself. I wanted the universe to be all-accepting, but one portion of the starry skies continued to draw away in disparagement or was simply unfriendly. Rivals were forthright in their desires to demean whatever I achieved. It was an indication of substance, John Gill said, that I caused the disquiet of so many. A wonderful, finally cathartic thing happened one day while I was sitting in the university student union. A climber told me about Pat Ament, not knowing that Pat Ament was the person to whom he was speaking: "I've seen Ament climb. He's not that good." History would not vindicate me, with regard to the negative judgments, nor would my own defensiveness absolve me—for the reason that, by definition, the inaccuracies were only partly false. Yet climbing endured, with different degrees of conviction, in its best part always light and good. It brought to me mature, responsible interchanges as a teacher of climbing where I was able to help others and where my love for climbing passed through their experience. They felt my spirit, and I theirs.

Somehow things didn't seem random. There was something vital in the way things opposed, one day enemies rooting for your demise, then days, weeks, that produced the opposite theme: to be able to love and impress your friends, to be a direct help to them, times which were the antithesis of evil, with trails, forest, existence consumed, in open, penetratingly-lit space where events conferred upon one his talents or informed him of them, and you were inspired, and people were allies. One climbed with the right feel of the sequences, led by a frail, higher rock that was provocatively compliant.

These were things one could not show or say in slides at a conference. In England I seemed to reflect on the entire memory of my climbing. Fresh, temperate winds that blew warmly across white, exquisite rock of El Capitan in summer. Sitting in starlight on a ledge on Sentinel Rock in Yosemite. Brown, perfect rock of Tuolumne, above Yosemite. Sunscreen on Higgin's nose, the wear along the sole of his shoe where he stood on footholds or edged against bright, celestial, knobbed rock. I thought of the Utah desert, climbs with Royal Robbins up Shiprock and Castleton Tower, the terror of rappels from red summits in the dark. Young climbing friends—Christian, tubing a river with him, Cam placing me on a skateboard at night to experience unrestrained speed, Gray's wide smile, thirteen-year-old, eighty pound, asthmatic Jeff as he dared the Yellow Spur of Eldorado with me, the breath-enhancing adrenalin of that route's exposed, vertical sandstone.

Places in Colorado, up walls of the Black Canyon of the Gunnison, doing the Crack of Fear above Estes Park, its sleek, diabolical appeal, and the sheer Diamond wall of Longs Peak. Ptarmigan walked alongside you in the tundra. That mountain's dark patterns of weather, and cold, morning earthshine. Quietly outclassed by Gill on boulders but finding in him perhaps my most understanding friend. The monolithic flatiron rocks above Boulder, their purple-hued light, lilac smells, when I was young and awe-struck by sandstone's immense, beguiling beauty, how rock expressed the idea, and then how the world of climbing began, abducted into the green of pines, the breath-mind of a breeze, meadows, inhalings, a silence, or eaglet's squeal from a ledge. A sling lightly weighting your collarbone, a twitch of chalk on an eyelash. There was the desire to persuade people to agree with you, or sometimes you wished you were more like everyone else, at times a search for the secrets of popularity—but the gold at the end of the rainbow was closer to what you valued in your friends. At a decision point, a cloud going across, you considered the karma that was building up in your life, a notion of regret, then movement upward, unbrilliant, sufficient, ecstatic, unforeseeing, a path that, with its extraordinarily beautiful configurations, defied the vicissitudes of life and seemed to override the earthly annoyances you knew. Ledges that you obtained after another profitless job. You seemed to see yourself in the surroundings, which made you feel coarse, and bare. Strange judgments led you uncannily to positions that you tried to avoid. Rock that seemed to offer a power. Rock on which an ability would come forward all at once when a section of climbing unexpectedly revealed its difficulty. Endless, telling incidentals.

Now a cloud—meandering, dropping around Snowdon. The dark projection of the mountains—I was their transient guest, invited into the interior of a land that by itself could re-create the aspirations of a spirit.

The pungence, the flow, its strong, forward rush—like time. The extraordinary darkness of night. I thought of the English writer Chesterton's description of life as "humiliating splendor," and his phrase, "...the abiding childhood of the world." I recalled how at the festival Dennis, seeing me with Bonatti, inquired half-jokingly if I was sharing some of my "screwed-up philosophy."

Snowdon mountain had grown as beautiful as a world could be. If there was something honest in the world it was a tree, a gull, a rare dotterel, it was light on the talus, or a fragrance of sea over yellow-orange heather, where the stupid things with which people could concern themselves, where both the littleness and the grandioseness of existence, could be dispelled. The mountains, the night, and stars, were, as I saw them, ways that a person's hold on attention, on honesty, enlarged—for fear of that circumstance to which one might easily relapse: cramped, despairing, less happiness for more effort, where there was no connection with the natural environs, where everyone appeared as though they were a notch above, or below, and friendship did not survive, and there was no feeling of psychic union.

Brede's simple, unmodernized house, ventilated by breezes, expressed its consciousness, a house's ration of time, light, and cold, a house left somewhat alone through the centuries.

My mind was still going when I thought I would droop from fatigue and sentimental melancholy.

I thought about an extensive graveyard that we had driven past—dark, tall crosses. Their color appeared to blow as wind, a tint of both exaltation and of oblivion. The fright of our human limits. The gratifying feeling of our human limits. I had thoughts of love toward all of my friends—whomever, wherever. At what point would I deal cheaply with one of them again?

Imagination, like language, could not have only a single theme, or be at one topic at a time. Mountains were a life of forms that took a person's body as well as his mind, his feeling as well as knowledge, asserting demands upon his resources as a giving, seeing individual. England's prose fiction, shepherds, poets, tales told in verse in castle halls. I thought about the smell of wind and wood, how in America they bulldozed houses that became a little old. The glorious planets and winds, the sky, ocean, cliffs, the incredible principle of imagination, in a way were weakened by reflection. There could be too many insights. The little renunciations of self, our eternal pursuit of vanishing ideals, and the seeming presence in us of some far-off life.... I felt that I had come, to a degree, for a few days, to that far-off life, to a remote conversation in a land that had been for me, until now, a thought.

It was gratifying to feel that you could transcend old spheres of feeling and could let a new purity well up in your life, a new mystery and splendor, in a small, august country. Out in the yard's quiet pasturage, I felt a lot of negativity leave me. I could see the faces of friends. Life had to be more than a series of blithe, optimistic steps antecedent to some regretful, black end you were unable to avert. The prayer was, for me, of a wider sense, a meaning arising from perhaps love. I had friends who were devout atheists or just rather earnestly irreverent. The research of their particular genius was greedily mortal, consumed on the happinesses of the moment. Their cynicism could be very refreshing, and usually I saw something spiritual in them if they didn't.

It was exactly in this fertile, contradictory, open-ended garden of thought that many of the most positive connections between experience, friendship, and climbing were made. There were no real goals in climbing. The rain-cold ledges of Whillans and Brown, their top hats and motor scooters, were now a myth. No matter what climbers achieved this day in the way of advanced abilities, somehow it could not hold great significance. Climbing writer Tom Patey once used the phrase "secluded laugh," an excellent description, I thought, of a cosmic insight that came for a climber as one of his better rewards. Long, mantis-thin, child contortionists with fingers as strong as ever now climbed lines on rock that required weeks of trying, haunted by dreams, to succeed. I was not the kind who, when he saw what he wanted, would never rest until he got it. That's what it took today to cherub among the stars. More and more I found myself sneaking past the start of obvious test climbs and continuing on to climbs that appealed for their deceptively difficult-looking but actually reasonable—with good technique—natures, climbs where the runouts between points of protection were shorter. It was providence to be invited here among some of the oldest, most aesthetically remarkable of such climbs.

Wales had that etheric metamorphism of a dream: cold, undulatory, lovely, dark, mysterious, calming to a rhapsodic mind. Yet being here for the first time was exhausting—the travel, the festival, the climbing, and meeting people, the constant giving of oneself, attempting to communicate, to hear, see, remember. I was shown to my bedroom, a tiny, private loft upstairs.

In the middle of the night, I woke up with anxiety. For many years I have had inexplicable attacks of fear. To describe what happens, there is a brief moment that is what you imagine insanity to be—a horrible terror that reduces everything to survival, a pure, almost total despair so frightening that it can only be diffused by a type of ego-death, an absolute acceptance of whatever doom. This all occurs in seconds, then is gone. Perhaps the true terror is that the fear will continue past its usual few seconds or take place in some location of no escape, such as climbing—where you might decide to unrope and jump, an unplanned but necessary suicide. It was characteristic of my imagination to exaggerate the possibilities. But here was one of those moments of strange, intense realization, or whatever it could be called, disoriented in my small, perfectly black loft, unable to remember in a few glances where I was. Would this be the attack that did not subside? Friends had said I was a controlled person, that I had a tight hold on "reality." They saw it in drawings that I did. It was true in physical ways, such as climbing or gymnastics. I was not crazy, nor was I unstable, as such fear suggested. I had learned to live with these huge, uncomfortable thrills. This one made me think how far I was from my home on another side of the Atlantic. I let myself envision an all-encompassing panic. Why did I have these bouts? Had I damaged myself from my small experiment with psychedelics in the '60s? Was there serious conflict in me that was unresolved? Good and evil at war within? Climbing seemed minor compared to the more serious perils of mind and soul. The few seconds abated, as always, and I was silenced by oblivion for the night.

In the morning Brede fed us, then took us to the little Welsh town of Llanberis, to Joe Brown's climbing shop where I bought a warmer shirt made of polypropylene. Brede walked me by the ear to a nearby bank to change some money—my excuse of having only dollars was quickly remedied. At the post office I eavesdropped on two Welsh women, the first asking how the other's husband was, and the second replying, "Seneeelity." The shirt I bought had Brown's name on it, and the bag it came in had his motto, "Don't look down, contact Joe Brown." We were not able to meet him, because he was fishing.

Brede introduced us to Martin Cook, a young climber, calm-spirited, who had thoughts of girls, pubs, climbs, and studying English with Jim Perrin. Jim had a Ph.D. in English biography. Brede chauffeured Martin, Charlie, and me to the angular, shattered outcrops of Tremadog, near the town of the same name. The rocks were set up against a hill. Very tall, slender trees obscured the bottom third of the wall. Sorting gear before starting off, Martin suggested that I bring one "friend" for use in a particular crack. I asked if one would be enough. In deja vu affrontery, Charlie intruded, "Joe Brown didn't use friends." I thought that Joe Brown didn't use wire stoppers, chalk, Fire shoes, or perlon rope—Charlie had them all. We approached Brown's gargoyle Vector—three excellent rope-lengths of steep, gray rock. The first section was coated lightly by a green, dangerously moist moss which maximized our attention on even moderately sized footholds. We moved up rock, behind the trees—maybe birch, they had white, peeling bark. Our fingers hurt and went dead from the cold—a numb, talon feeling—and then really stung for a few minutes when they warmed up. I remembered other climbers say they enjoyed cold and pain. I would always be suited to warm Colorado sandstone in summer. A fern grew out of a crack. At one position, Charlie wanted to hang on tension from the rope in order to take a photo looking down at Martin and me. I noted, "Joe

Brown would not have hung on tension." It bothered me that Charlie was not more unlikeable. I could not lie to myself as to who was the more intrepid leader. He was younger, more desire, fewer interests outside of climbing, his glories mostly still ahead, mine lost in the benign memory of a culture. Who was it — Shaw? — who said that society destroyed its heroes? Charlie balanced a sling delicately on a horn of rock, clipped a carabiner to it and the rope through the carabiner. Marginal protection, but the moves were wholly before his eyes. He came to an anvil-forged, fossil piton which the angel of death had passed over. When it was my turn to climb, belayed by Charlie, I was stiff. My Helly-Hansen coat felt like a suit of armor. I moved up under a huge, overhanging blade of rock that was a legendary feature of the route and the side of which you had to ascend. It was really intimidating here, your body forced into a tilt to the right, making the delicate tops of the trees point up at you from the right. If I fell, I would be caught by the rope but would leave the rock and swing quite far outward into space near those treetops. This was probably one of the climbs Brown had led in a full rain. My fingers reached into a crack, and it was filled with damp soil. I tried to find leverage or balance or cross-pressure but, as it turned out, had to just climb it.

Runouts being what they are, I didn't mind this one being Charlie's. As I followed, I had none of the helpful adrenalin that flows by the act of leading.

On the last pitch I led over a roof, out of sight from my companions, and focused on the wall above — steep, less gray. Suddenly I was on a headwall, off route — as evidenced by Brede who, below on the road, shouted and gesticulated with her arms. Climbing was like heroin. You were lost if you had even a germ of desire. I reversed the moves, amassing a lot of slack in the rope. "Take in the rope," I asked. Up rose the voice of the curmudgeon: "Go for it," as though to say, "What do you think this is, a holiday?" It began to drizzle. I went for it. A traverse left, a lieback on a flake, aggressively to the top. Charlie followed and, at one move, called to me, "Up rope." I echoed him, "Go for it." From the summit, we could see the distant town of Tremadog, chimney pots, the Irish Sea, sky breaking up clear. A wide, green meadow spread out below and in front of us. A train passed through the meadow, through green, exquisite, showery daylight. On the rim of the rock where we stood, a sheep had grazed to us via its own route. It stared at us through an opening between two bushes, its lower jaw moving in a circle.

We were not that much higher than the delicate boughs of the trees, the route a means to Brown's time, the big blade sticking out, shadowed in clouds of time and sky. Along the road below was Eric Jones' climbing cafe toward which we descended, at tea time.

We returned to Brede's, to food, warm drink, chess, and my card tricks that failed to fool the kids. We listened to the music of "Clash," an English punk group. Brede's eldest daughter, a borderline punker, was voluptuous, hair black and long. One of the girls had a birthday. Some trick candles were used that lit again after being blown out. That night, I wondered if Charlie's and my gloom would persist or if friendship would shine again in its first temper of sun. I took my station in the loft.

Morning came coldly. Brede drove us to the coast—Holly Head and Gogarth—where walls of quartzite rose thrillingly out of the ocean, where wind and rain kept us from serious ascents. Wet, grass trails led us, freezing, tottery, along the brinks of cliffs—one slip away from a fall hundreds of feet to the waves. Mother of eight, Brede climbed fearlessly. She led us on, the rock blustery, dizzily far above the water. She pointed to a line of gulls "queuing up" in single file on a ledge. With flutters in our stomachs we traversed out to the ends of Being, on ledges went unroped eerily above the ocean, rain continuing to "bucket down," as Brede phrased it. We were soon frozen, soaked by sleet, and ignoring it. It seemed to be the order of the day to suffer the cold but enjoy the dream. We bouldered above crashing, story-telling foam. Brede told of a climber who, while bouldering at the bottom of the cliff, was taken away by a larger than usual wave and was never seen again.

Drying out in a restaurant, Charlie and I got into it once more. He listed the defects, integritywise, that I had demonstrated over the years as a climber. The rain stopped as we left the cafe. I felt the chill of the fresh streets, the smell of damp grass, and the soothing accord of the trees. That evening, I ignored my rib and vengefully created three short dynamic climbs on the indoor wall where Brede trained. Charlie, shorter than I, was daunted by the reaches. Next morning, in Llanberis, he bickered with me about a roll of film I had borrowed. We retired to a corner of Pete's Eats, another climbing cafe, and really had it out, reduced to verbally abusing one another. He suggested that I (who he had called the "master crack climber") wasn't a very good climber. I proposed an alteration in the location of his nose. Martin and some others quietly minded their own business at a table across the room. It must all have met with their approval. Someone said later that our friendship had the scandalous aspect of true English friendships, that a measure of verbal brawling, a "row," showed our true spirits. Perhaps it was the simple clash of Charlie's Scotch grain and my Irish. At a point of peak anger, silence, end of friendship forever, we drove with Martin to Llanberis Pass where Charlie and I caught sight again of Cenotaph Corner—frightful, no rain, no mist, nothing shrouding it. We were possessed with the idea of climbing it. Martin dropped us off, and we hiked, hurried, desultory, up the scree slope, in no apparent disagreement, haunted once again by some choreography happening on the vertical inner walls of our minds.

When we reached the base, the corner was filled with slime from weeks of rain and made us turn to its more difficult but dryer Left Wall. Although moist at its top, this latter possibility seemed reasonable and even more attractive, a blessing in disguise. It was a route which proved to be incredible, pure, delicate, singular, a thin crack slicing a hundred and sixty feet of sheer, flat, vertical rock. We flipped a ten pence for the lead. Part way up that lead, my fingers cold and arms getting tired, I said, "Guess you're right, Charlie, I can't climb very well." He disagreed vehemently, replying, "You better be careful what you say to your belayer." The middle part of the route forced me into a series of wide stems— doing the splits between providentially-located extrusions of rock.

One did not usually fall off the rock, but sometimes we fell inward, or bounced off one another. Climbing was valuable in part because it transcended the directions you thought you were going. There was gratification derived from the power of your own body. You worked your way up places of rock and reveled in them. I wondered if people were still talking about us at Pete's Eats. This was climbing, one of the most unboring things a person could do—fresh, vernal air suggesting youth and spring, hills vintage green, rock with hinted-at routes. Anachronistic castles. Eternally dated rock rising now in twentieth century light, crags of those independent, early, virtuoso rock mates.

Rock was a constituent of the culture, a romanticism. It was emotion. The arcane. The lonely. The magical. It was a person way up where I was, ready to fight, irreducible, the way Howard Nemerov once described poetry, "A fairytale in which you are not permitted to ask how it is done." My mind held the image of a huge, gray, leafless tree I had seen when Jim, Charlie, and I arrived in Wales. Much of climbing was this kind of personal inventory. The rock was a poetry, with you as its limited audience. The world had other things on its mind, and just as well.

My eyes were up close to the rock's deformed, textured gray. Rock hewn sheer. Water covered the thinnest, most difficult part of the crack. Where I could let go with one hand, I set a nut and pulled on it—permissible to get past the water. My fingers stung as life kindled in them. I crushed the tips of them into the crack, found a tiny foothold, moved up. I belayed Charlie up. Hundreds of feet below, cars drove on the damp, fictive road of Llanberis Pass. For the moment I was on top of my quarrels with life. But it was a limited advantage. As I rappelled, the heavy, drenched rope kinked into a blob that would not slide through my hand. My hat was falling over my eyes. I tried to see through two slits in the yarn, as though the hat were a black hood, and I my own nooseman. I hung in space, my hands tiring severely, desperate to untwist the mess. I hoped that when I did untwist it I would not then, from fatigue, slide off the end of the rope and sail out of sight all the way down Llanberis Pass. Charlie couldn't see me where I was: pinioned on the wall just right of Cenotaph Corner. I suppose it was an inopportune time to study the size of the holds in the corner, to notice a fixed sling, and to imagine climbing the route, but I was doing that while at the same instant struggling to survive. I swung into the corner and with the help of a wrist through that fixed sling unsnarled the rope. I finished the rappel, Charlie came down. I said nothing about getting hung up. We descended and had a long American discussion in a grassy, autonomous meadow, rain relaxing onto our knuckles, and far above: the exalted, healing, great rock corner of Llanberis.

Martin not around, we hitch-hiked toward Brede's, feeling the English desire to be among friends. Charlie posed for a little photographic trickery, hitch-hiking on the correct side of the road for America. We caught a short ride with a woman who seemed to know about climbing and was impressed that we had climbed the left wall of Cenotaph Corner. She dropped us near Llanberis, a two mile walk from Brede's. Charlie walked faster, and I found myself removed enough from him to enjoy in a private way the utterly lovely Welsh country where trees, lakes, green, and varieties of blue seemed to be seen with a retrospect of centuries. Each leaf or ripple bore the difficulty of life, of what we knew, not only the breadth of human accomplishment but the depth of its failure. The

mountains were slightly somber under a day of clouds, yet beautiful. Little nests in trees. Was the world easier now than it was for
Keats or Coleridge? We related to experience glibly...the ways the
wildernesses were now pruned, a plenum of technologies, our
assumption of moving beyond the barbaric. Here in history, our
meanings were certainly...better? I imagined the delight of poetry
of earlier centuries, how individuals acknowledged the matters of
their day, an age of daggers and early death. We could thank them
for seeing that time for us, a time retained in oils and poetry and
no doubt exercising within us some genetic legacy. I envisioned
myself in lace and knickers, a feudal society's liege, the iron sound
of a portcullis being raised, voices of delicate ladies, people mind-
ful, enjoying the pleasures of food, of touch, of thought, feeling
life as it took them in, faithful, reflective, mad, or diseased, who in
an evening sun heard the water that now flowed. They felt the
same damp and darkness that I felt now.

I was struck by a desire to be with a woman, in each other's
arms, safe, warm, a tenderness, no distance between us, no
separateness. Unable to conjure a face, I felt she was beautiful. I
thought back to times in my life I had fallen in love, how easy it
happened always, each an isolated act. Where now? The oldest
sorrow of life was to awaken in a world and find that you were not
in love. Specifically in love, that is. My mind was serious and
satiric by turns, an energy that haled in every ravine, tree, bough,
every form, and perspective. Clouds drifted with psychotic beauty
across the sky.

The road grew steeper, and to exert was to compete with the
idle flow of the mind. As the road led higher onto the hill toward
Brede's, I looked back west at the Irish Sea which could be
discerned obscurely between gray-white, low-hanging clouds.
Hills, the coast, waves. Terns. A kittiwake. Its red legs. My
footsteps. The road. Heather. Field stock. Gentians. Sopping, yellow.

I embraced that beautiful woman, that ideal, seemed to possess
the animism of her soul.

At Brede's, I learned that Mirella had tried to reach me. Her
recorder had failed to capture the dialogue with Bonatti and me,
nor did it get the interview with me. She had taken a train to Wales,
waited for me, given up, and left for Italy. I would later receive a
letter from her: "Oh well, what right had I to be in possession of a
dialogue which was the encounter of two worlds, two souls. It has
been privilege enough to be the witness of that encounter and to

play the role of interpreter. I'm sure I did interpret you both, not only linguistically. And what you said wasn't so important, after all, but what was important was the discovery, the message, the feelings. In a way, I feel that the gods did right to destroy an evidence which was only half an evidence and to just leave the feelings intact. I translated your poem for Bonatti, and he was very moved by the intensity of your feelings."

Brede was mother, teacher, charmer, washed our underwear, showed us moves across the indoor wall. She repeatedly confused the name Charlie Fowler with a local comic character Charlie Farley, to Charlie's chagrin. At our parting, she handed me a canister of Barley Cup as a souvenir. I left a few pounds in British paper money under a cup on a mantelpiece.

Jim Perrin fetch us with his car and drove Charlie and me around narrow curves to a mysterious, gray-stone house. Above on a hill, was an old, uninhabited castle. The name of the house, "Tan Y Castell," was Welsh for "under the castle." First glance at the house in evening, it seemed sinister—the castle above silhouetted in a sky with clouds in turbulent, apocalyptic forms. Tan Y Castell would prove easy to love. Now in Jim's domain, he seemed warm and welcoming. I did not press the issue of his hesitancy at our meeting at the festival but thought of a positive letter he had sent to me prior to my coming to England: "Looking through your very fine book, it came home to me just how much what you write does resonate through my own experience: in the '60s for example (I started climbing at age 13 in 1960) I was a sort of protege of Crew and Boysen, perhaps the Brit versions of Robbins and Kor; then had a brief day in my own right, faded off into other pursuits for awhile, then started back in with a new generation with whom I could sometimes keep pace through guile, wrote about it continually, and there were the women of course, and keeping fit which gets harder year in, year out...must lobby here and there to try to get you as the guest for the Buxton Mountaineering Conference. If this comes off, we must get together for some bouldering, gritstone, spaghetti, and vitriolic, no-holds-barred, totally scurrilous praise-and-denunciation sessions that in this country go under the name of conversation."

Now was out ordained time to be together. A spaghetti feast introduced the stay at Tan Y Castell. Both of us Bob Dylan freaks from the '60s, Jim and I lounged about the fire regurgitating Dylan lyrics. Jim demonstrated almost photographic memory, the first person I had met who could recite Dylan as accurately as I. I challenged him to guess my favorite of the newer Dylan tunes. Without pause, he answered correctly, to my shock, "Lenny Bruce is Dead." Jim had fixed in his mind passages from Wordsworth and Yeats. His recall of literature was enviable. Vision in only one eye, long brown rebel hair flowing in tangled curls, soft-spoken, his voice slow and slightly falsettoed, Jim seemed to stare away into space—yet did not lack hearing. His wife Doris was attractive, their three children friendly to me and spirited. Teenage Vickie played the piano with me. Her younger brother Mark played chess with me, and tiny, wildly blonde-haired William pounced on me each morning with a yelp (both his and mine). Tan Y Castell was the exception to the rule. It was warm. Reputation had preceded me: Jim stoked a fire in at least two rooms. There was a shower. A wash basin was in the bathroom! I was not obligated to climb.

Jim gave us a slide show of some of his climbing in England.

Tan Y Castell stood among a few trees, quiet, in a valley, the outlands of Gwnedd, North Wales. A stream flowed on the north side of the house. A train ran through a meadow to the south. There were the soothing sounds of water, rails, sheep, breezes. Cars had only very narrow roads, the usual small, stone hedges laboriously built along the roads and as boundaries of property. In the area, bridges of stone rose from their ends to a point in the middle—architecture dating before Shakespeare. It seemed almost wrong to drive a car in these old places. Jim's house was a sixteenth century Methodist meeting hall, his study rich with wood, an old, well-tuned, upright piano calling from a corner. On Jim's desk sat a draft of his newest book—the biography of Menlove Edwards, a profound British climber, pioneer, writer, homosexual, and suicide. In the front yard rose a pointed marble spire, a monument twenty feet high, built in tribute to the early tenants of the house. The monument had inscribed on it, "Music, Poetry, Eloquence, Theology," terms of enduring relevance that seemed in any age to celebrate life. Jim's home was intellect, artistry, refinement, sensitivity. Along several walls were shelves filled with books, a house clean, unaffected. The first night here, after retiring to my sleeping bag on the floor of Jim's study, I had another dementia, waking from a dream into dark's sepulcher-like elegance. Where was I? I thought that I could feel the presence of those Methodist ghosts.

Some of the detail of Tan Y Castell: an armchair, a letter falling through a mail drop, half-burned bricks of coal sitting cold in the living room fireplace, a thrust of light through a window, the brisk, invigorating temperature of a morning, a lovely photo of Doris on a wall near Jim's desk, a hairpin of Vickie's, Jim staring into fresh flame in the kitchen fireplace, a crease in his shirtsleeve, the pink, sandy tongue of a cat. In the yard were glittery grasses, a wooden gate, swift clouds spaciously rolling about in the sky, a small flower garden, a white bird far away in a meadow of the countryside. The steam of a kettle. Cupboards, a fork, a jar of jam. These various objects and sights vibrated with the values of the people that they were near.

Jim prepared breakfast. Breakfast was the largest meal in Britain, usually a smorgasboard in one plate. Here were eggs, sausage, bacon, beans, bread, and fruit, then "drinking chocolate." Jim sat at a big wood table in the kitchen, sipped tea. He glanced at me as though to ask a question silently and try the adequacy of my silent answer.

Charlie found relief from me with two other climbers, Paul Williams and Pat Littlejohn. Like Charlie, they were keen, an affinity for the aims, the more climbs the better, the less reflection the more swordplay and derring do.

Jim drove me by the house of Lawrence of Arabia and a house where Shelley had lived, both in Tremadog. He spoke of Welsh miners and the area's failing economy. We did a steep climb on the Tremadog rocks with a gymnast and boxer named Mel. I tied into the rope and proceeded up through limbs and foliage, up a series of frail grass terraces clumped against the first sheets of the wall. Rock—I led up through its working-class slums, stopped and fidgeted with a nut, tried to place it in a horizontal crack, then arranged another nut in opposition to keep the first nut from falling out when I moved above. I glanced downward and could see Jim and Mel in a nice chat. My rope fed out from behind Jim's back and through his hands. I felt for a hold that was hidden around a corner to the right. I balanced around the corner, feet on tiny edges. Finger placements in a small crack up a vertical rock. Climbing was boys tossed into the air like pennies. It was old men moving slowly upward like petrified monsters. Jim huffed a little as I belayed him up. He apologized that he was getting over an illness. We descended along the rim of the rock which slowly angled down to the road. Someone took a photo of Jim and me as we sat '40s style on the bumper of a car, an arm over each other's shoulder.

That night, a potato casserole, followed by a British "dessert" of cheese and crackers, brought the Tan Y Castell family—Charlie, Jim, Doris, the cats, Jim's dog (curled up on Jim's lap), and me—to the television ("telly") to vanish into an offbeat Robert Mitchum western. No commercials to disrupt my senses, I dozed for a few minutes, unfortunately—Jim noted—during the crucial twist.

Human consciousness was a workshop where you were always half ready to concede. Implication, assessment, interpretation, response, defense. You were released into the shire of a world, into rapport and stimulus and suggestion. You spoke and heard, and then waited among the potentials. You let hopes build, hopes of friendship, for example. On a brief return to England two years later, I would find Jim distant, inwardly involved, and distracted by the imminent death of an older friend of his.

The next day, Jim and I climbed two routes at Carreg Alltrem, a wall of rock above the small, blue village of Dolwyddelan, very near Jim's house. Catching sight of Carreg Alltrem, I made a comment that the cliff looked steep. Jim explained that my words were interesting since "Carreg Alltrem" meant "the steep looking rock." After a short approach that led mystically upward through a forest, past a stream and makings of spring, we climbed the Lavaredo Wall. "You'll like this climb, Patrick, it's about 5.7!" He described us as geriatric hippies. We climbed very steep rock, with good holds, joys that invited talk. Jim laughed, quoted Wordsworth. He had many quotes: "In the country of the blind, the one-eyed man is king" (H.G. Wells) and "Whoever perpetually strives, those only can we help" (the good angel to Faust). Perrin seemed a bit of a Faust himself, certainly having sold a little of his soul for knowledge. Snowflakes flew around his head in two-minute storms, the sun never leaving. We climbed, with the simple desire to enjoy. A raven warned us of a nest nearby. Perrin looked a bit how I imagined Poe—as though "...he had been alone/ Amid the heart of many thousand mists" (Wordsworth), thin, an indefinable, slightly diabolical smile. We climbed another route. Jim's black dog watched from below. High on Carreg Alltrem I found a Bonatti carabiner, just one more cosmic momento—abandoned on a sling, apparently by climbers who retreated in a storm.

By the fire, I read Jim's new book—the Menlove biography. The book was a daring effort, marked by its compassion. Charlie read a climbing guide. Jim sat down beside Doris. He groaned from too much dinner. As I read, I thought that writing filled for Jim and me the need of an organizing principle in our lives. We used words to work out our lives. At nearby Capel Curig, a pub and headquarters of the Welsh climbing club, I gave a slide show.

Jim introduced me to the small audience as "...the States' most creative climbing pen." Afterward, as I entered the pub, one John Barry was virtually shouting at Jim, arguing some point that seemed not only ridiculous but insulting. I heard Barry call Jim "extremist." A few people considered Jim a threat, in part because of his political-ecological activism. Jim deplored the poisoning of the environment and destruction of ancient land, edifices, and culture, and he had weird affiliations, such as with the Communist Party in England. It struck me that Jim's pursuits had to do with his intelligence — inquisitive, active.

Jim mildly exited the room, subdued, perhaps angry. I followed. On the drive to his house, we brooded about people. He related to me that John Barry, who criticized him at Capel Curig, disliked me also and thought that I must be gay because of my following of younger climbers. We noted that I had friends my own age and older. We spoke of friendship, its spontaneity, the quality, the desperateness, how society tended to resent friendship. In Shakespeare's time, friendship between men was a rare, valued thing spoken of openly as love. Since then, society had changed. Said Samuel Johnson, "Friendship, peculiar boon of heaven,/ The noble mind's delight and pride:/ To men and angels only given,/ To all the lower worlds denied." Rhymey, but it addressed the issue.

It was difficult to recognize the worth of others and not be limited in our estimation of what others had to offer. I was no saint in these tasks but felt that I was making efforts to improve.

At home we learned that Don Whillans had phoned, wondering which pub we would be at. I wanted only to sleep, even to experience terror — then to be soothed by a dream of a river or a train.

The next day was Jim's birthday, but he and Doris had to attend the funeral of his aunt. Charlie was off again with some climbers. I needed a day by myself, explored the castle on the hill above Jim's house. I climbed its stairwells, examined the stone as though to draw history from it in small, fogged abridgments. Thoughts stirred the mud and death of time, instilling in me feelings of the brevity — but also the eternity — of life. By foot I visited the Welsh village of Dolwyddelan. As a birthday present for Jim, I purchased a small, delicate bowl made of blown glass, intricately designed, its glass blue. I imagined that the color of the glass would be received by his single, richly exploring eye. The children baked a cake. That night, we had Jim's birthday party. He seemed quiet, more so than usual, perhaps thinking of his aunt. These candles did not re-light. Outside were the stars, the air cold. It would soon be time to leave this house, Tan Y Castell, set below a castle in the sky. Jim suggested that I stay longer, but I was directed by some unknown itinerary from within, "Swift as a shadow, short as any dream"—Shakespeare.

In the morning, Jim handed me, as a gift, a descriptive English novel from his shelves, called The Pathway. Jim, Charlie, and I drove to Craig Y Forwyn, a limestone cliff in North Wales, to deliver us back to Ken Wilson but first to climb huge, scary overhangs. A local climber belayed my rope as I led out backwards, underneath Mojo Roof, my body leaning under the great roof and then moving over it. I ascended a steep wall to the top of the cliff, and Charlie followed as I belayed him. Our troubles gone, our climbing sharpened its focus on the features of rock. Jim walked lazily below, taking photos. I sat belaying atop the cliff and gazed out at the green, easy, country hills. Ken arrived at the top of another climb nearby.

"Show us some more technical wizardry," he taunted, explaining to me the errors of my ways. Jim's slight voice drifted up, "Give 'm hell, Ken." Ken interjected a compliment about my ease on Mojo Roof.

Toward the end of afternoon, I started but failed to lead another overhang. As Ken belayed me, I tried to set a small nut in a crack I could only feel above the lip of the overhang. To do this I had to hang from one arm, my sore arm, too long and lost confidence in being able to do the lead with any margin of control. I clipped a carabiner and my rope to the nut. The journey, I thought, had sung its ballad, when disappointment was satisfying and so many scrambled things added up. It felt unnecessary to try. I dangled from my arms, mute, inert, having no will or power or motion or endurance. One or two excuses hazarded in the presence of Charlie and the others, I lowered to the ground. Charlie did the lead with predatory zeal. I thought that he had been my opposition during the trip, a kind of foil, as in literature—to provide contrast. I watched several eager others, including a man in his fifties, move (with the benefit of a top rope) somewhat effortlessly up the route. Jim expressed concern about my arm and rib and did not view them as excuses but rather as obstacles I was attempting to overcome. Jim made it past the difficult protrusion of rock but then was reluctant to go higher on moves he should have been able to do.

At a pub, I bought myself a lemonade and Jim a shandy. Outside I embraced Jim, shook his hand, said farewell. The figure of Jim Perrin was lost in the dark, as I walked away.

Charlie and I would part here too, Charlie deciding to go to France with several climbers. On the long drive east with Ken to his home in Macclesfield, I thought about Jim Perrin. There was something in those insignificant climbs. Part of the value was as sentences — the way you listened to them later. Ken clamored on about any subject, however inconsequential. A book/climbing magazine editor, he was also a lover of jazz. As we sped toward Macclesfield, we listened to Noel Coward on the radio. The song's words had surprising appropriateness: "We're going to untense our muscles 'til they sag sag sag." Ken's house was a large, two-story, red-brick structure with trees and a lush park for a backyard. He served me cocoa, insisting that cocoa was an aphrodisiac. I wasn't certain why I should need one. Through Ken I learned more uses of the British word "piss": "Getting pissed" (drowning in beer), "Pissing" (the rain"), "Pocket pissing" (where climbers complimented each other's achievements, favors which, as understood, were to be returned). Although very intelligent, Ken had a brazenness, disrupting organizations and meetings and hoity-toity denizens of the land.

Morning came. Ken's black wife Gloria and I discussed the Buxton talks. Ken's eldest (twelve-year-old?) son and I played the piano together. I wondered how they tolerated Ken. They were calm, content.

I would take a train today to London. Ken calculated that we could fit in a fast few hours of climbing at The Roaches, near the hermit's house in Staffordshire where I'd begun. It was a day of sun, yet also those peculiar flurries of snow coming briefly from nowhere and then vanishing. Nearby, The Sloth jutted out ominously.

"Geeee, these British climbs are real neat," Ken said mocking me. As we hiked toward the Third Cloud formation, he said, "In a little bit you'll be able to see the crack...winking at you. It's a real winker."

He took my camera and began raving about how drab, how pitifully, I was dressed, and ordered me to roll up my pants a little and pull back my shirtsleeves for better photographic definition against the rock. "Keep that hat off, it makes you look like an old woman," he said sharply. In a flurry of snow, he followed my lead of a vertical finger crack and noted, "That was really bloody hard, with cold fingers. It makes it so good when there's a little sun kissing the rock," and, looking for a handhold, "Where's the jooog (jug)?!" The sun kept shining in and out, and I felt happy. I noticed a very small, lone cottage near a tree, by itself in a heather. The cottage overlooked an infinity of green and its lakes. Ken observed, "This climb is real nice." Curious if he was mocking me again, I asked, "Is that American or British?" He replied slowly, "That's about...mid-Atlantic."

I climbed away from the reach of his sounds, except that they were loud enough to indubitably flow: "Try not to place those friends too much, a good nut feels more honest!"

He raced the car home, around dangerous, single-lane curves, down narrow, stoned-rimmed roads. He was oblivious to the possibility of an unseen, onrushing car and hurried to make sure I caught my train before I was assimilated into the national identity.

At his house he fixed another cocoa aphrodisiac for me, and we drove to my train.

A swift train rocked and slanted southward to London. A last stop in Oxted remained, a visit to some friends and hopefully a last glance at London. On the underground (the British subway), a man standing beside me said, "A couple of minutes and we'll be passing directly under Buckingham Palace. If you look up, you may catch a glimpse of the queen." At the next station, he walked with me to make sure I found my connection. On the final brief train ride to Oxted, the conductor noticed that among my things was a rope. He asked, "Been climbing?" I nodded in the affirmative, and he said, "My school teacher once took a climbing party into the mountains of Wales." He punched my ticket, then — after about a minute — added, "Oh, and 'e came back successfully as well." While on the train, I caught sight of a woman, the first serious possibility for "death-devouring love" (unless it would have been Brede's sixteen-year-old, dark-haired, pale, punker beaut). I remained aloof, imagining the transatlantic phone bill and deciding that this woman was, besides too beautiful, haunted. The English were ghoulish for lack of sun. In the night, at a stop, I watched a couple of station workers slowly unload bags of mail in what seemed despairing monotony, men dressed in black sailor coats, not talking. They were thinking, perhaps counting hours or minutes, the days until a pay, balancing their budgets in their minds, not necessarily wishing they had been born into privilege but rather thinking of quitting-time and a pub.

I phoned my friends at Oxted—Adrian and his wife Tracy. They were astonished at my timing: a tape they had of my piano music was playing on their stereo. I got off the train at a stop about two doors from their apartment. They fed me, prepared a scalding bath. We stayed up late. I shared with them a few of the details of my trip, the Edlinger shoes, the various people assigned to friendship me, posted like sentinels along the way, the waitress who called me "luv." There were a few ironies, for example that the trip had required the perfect amount of money to leave me with none at the end.

The final morning filled itself with London, watching people, a stop for pastries with Adrian, a visit to a climbing shop to find a pair of Scarpa climbing shoes for my young Colorado friend Gray. He had given me money to buy them for him. We passed a movie house, on the marquee: "Blood Bath At The House Of Death." We visited the tranquil grounds of a Mormon temple.

Then I was on the plane, looking out a window at takeoff. I recalled my anxieties before the trip, recalled Geraldine (the girl we had climbed with at Stanage), her repeated British, "Right, then." I recalled a night at Brede's where I overheard Brede counsel her young son to say his prayers and that they would make his illness go away.

It bothered me that I hadn't returned Whillans' phone call.

Climbing—bizarre, but a profound source of joy, discovery, comedy, a benefactor to those of us to whom it belonged. The deeper one entered, the more that existed—art, people, their natures. Climbing was more than moving hands or feet on rock. It could be a short, meditative walk in starlight in a Welsh land, or a feel of sky while on rock, a soul talking in a black universe. You could be stirred by the slate texture of gritstone. Such rock was simple in the way it was ennobling. Eyes took in the light. A mind consulted different holds. Repose, hesitation, inwardly seeing the rock, the wind, sky, a tree, a lone cottage, the dialect of shadows. The phenomenology of climbing—given moments. Fresh, oxygenated air. The Roaches, a hermit, palaces of stone half hidden. Moss. Green. Climbers edging up slowly, sometimes indifferently. Small, emotive voices as though coming from England's asylums. Climbing, I thought, was ground for self-esteem, or for supposing a progression in ourselves, depending, as in the arts, on the rarity of the experience and on the integrity of the response.

The plane shot upward. I had found no time to set my watch—still showing Colorado time. I was Arlo's sailor "...sailing over Jordan on the road back home again." There were feelings to be left behind, pockets empty, no jingling coins. I had my Bonatti carabiner. I had "Music, Poetry, Eloquence, and Theology." From the plane, England shrank. The moors, mists, foam moved into the past. There would not be the same England again, or people, Ian, Dennis, Ken, Brede, Mirella, Charlie Farley, and Sloth—the beauty queen. Walter, ciao. Good flight, Carreg Alltrem raven. Fare thee well, Tan Y Castell. Jim, remember Dylan, and remember Wordsworth: "Man, if he do but live within the light of high endeavors, daily spreads abroad his being with a strength that cannot fail."

*Writing under a pseudonym is something that may be neces-
sary to the actively-published writer, to keep from over-submit-
ting and being resented. I have not written under a pseudonym
very many times. I enjoyed the research and psychopathorama
required to create the following diary, published in The Climbing Art, 1988. Not a mountaineer, I suppose this story reflects
what I imagine (somewhat cynically) that most expeditions are
about.*

The First Ascent of Everest

by Captain Nicolino Kloche Rubini

(A translation from the Italian)

16 March. Perhaps I am here too early. But I am bound in my
ambition, determined to achieve the victory, my dream. George
Mallory and his companion Andrew Irvine did some learning that
will serve us. If we shall die, as they, if we're entitled, if we choose
so, after giving it a fight, or if the gods decide, then we will. I do
not believe in these gods.

Above Mallory's "Second Step," at least, there are no gods.
Nothing exists at that height, no oxygen, no breath, no hope, no
comfort. Perhaps reason itself must cease to happen in the thin,
deadly cold. Does one simply collapse in despair? Do not doubt
yourself, Nicolino.

I would have preferred an approach through Tibet, more difficult logistically but we would go entirely unnoticed. Instead I
must visit again the villages of the Solo Khumbu, be worshiped or
asked to worship at the monastery of Thyangboche. I am a godless
soul. I am confused among the many languages—Hindi, Urdu,
Nepali, Garhwall, Punjabi, Yalmo. The Sherpa are an enigmatic
race. Wood shingled roofs. The open windows (no glass) in Namche Bazar.

From Calcutta we have come through India by train, as far as
Raxaul, then by lorry through the jungle foothills to Bimpedi.
Then by foot we reached the valley of Nepal, and Katmandu.

Hindu-Buddhist temples. Bright green fields. Rice. The wild, shaggy yak. The pastures. "Thuji chey" (I am grateful), a Sherpa said to me today. Everest is known to them as Chomolungma. I prefer the name Everest because it is easier to say. In mountaineering, the easiest is always better. We have resorted to flagrant bribery and used some lies to get the help of the authorities. We are "ecological explorers." Our ropes are brought for river crossings. Our tanks of oxygen are brought because we're hopeless weaklings over 15,000 feet. They drink these gross absurdities as readily as I am asked to drink the harsh Tibetan tea they sweeten with a rancid butter of the yak.

17 March. The sight of an elusive, red panda.

The local porters aid us. Tremendous loads to carry. We use headstraps to further support our burdens. Thar Phuka, we agree, must be sirdar to Ajiba and the others of the Sherpa. We shall be forced to leave these friends before we start on Everest and send them back, that they do not detect our purposes too visibly. Integrity would not let them be altogether blind.

In the steep valley between the great mountains of Tawache and Ama Dablam, children tend to yaks. A yak has fallen on its side, loaded with our provisions.

19 March. The beginning of the Khumbu Glacier. Base camp soon, at 16,000 feet. The porters bid adieu. We are to begin our "ecology." We are alone now, the four of us. The wind is very bad this evening. The tents shake like sheets hung on a line. It is important that we have arrived prior to the British who I have learned shall be led by Hunt. I am informed that they are trained, that they are accompanied by a climber from New Zealand. I have learned from a member of the Ghang La family of the Sherpa that the British expedition shall employ a Tenzing Norgay. A Sherpa, born upon the Himalaya, in a village, is acclimatized already. Norgay has been on Everest before, in 1952 , with Lambert. They reached 27 or 28,000 feet, if I recall. I cannot forget Mallory's description of Everest as "a prodigious white fang excrescent from the jaw of the world."

My mind ambles through these events of history: Mallory, Irvine, dead in the early 1920's, they did not return from high on the mountain. Maurice Wilson, dead in 1934, the Russians in '52, and Eric Shipton who retreated in 1951. Tilman, Houston. They doubted, thus they failed.

I find myself partially haunted by a rather lovely Indian woman by the name of, if I have it correct, Ang Lahm who we passed, and who tried to portend to us, in a village. She showed a quietly disturbing (and unsolicited) curiosity about our exploits.

21 March. Afternoon. I stop again to write, to enter in my diary whatever piece of texture that I can, to note and to record and to remember. High wind. In the sunlight. One's companions are the instruments of his success, each a member of a cruel, social fabric, little more. This may seem ruthless. It's no secret I am ruthless. My team is chosen carefully, because they can withstand. We all are ruthless, godless, and expendable.

It is an ordeal to move forward at this altitude. The summit remains far away, the wind is terribly cold. It is the pre-monsoon, yet the weather, I fear, is not conventional, very ominous for this time of year.

22 March. The wind has been lashing our tents, keeps us from sleeping. I boil water for tea. I eat but am incessantly hungry. This could result in a shortage of food. Our food must last the necessary time.

Hind is beginning already to complain of the weather conditions, and I am tired of him. I think he is a coward. I explain to him that there cannot be good weather in a place such as this, that we are a part of an adventure. He is moody, a short sleeper. I have noticed that he is not a vigilant guide. He set out to find a route through the Icefall and returned, a ghost as pale as the snow. He had gotten lost between the first walls of the Icefall, unable to identify the route of his return and narrowly surviving the collapse beneath his feet of a hidden snow bridge. His ice axe luckily caught him on the other side of the void which otherwise would have swallowed him.

Gratchbur is a gregarious idiot. He philosophizes about comradeship. I do not feel any notion of a comradeship. His romance will kill him. He was never this romantic, it seemed, before. The altitude is likely getting to us all. He is paranoid, he's losing strength. He is in a state of degeneration, before my eyes. It is a macabre stare.

Agathos is quite strong, of note his work on rock, but I am finding him discouraged as a mountaineer. He searches with his heart for rock to climb. As he examines route possibilities he is attracted in his imagination to the rock, to steepness, rather than to the simple couloir which is there before him. On the mountain, the easiest way is always the way. I shall not allow him to be the death of me.

When the storm subsides, we shall examine the route more wisely. I stop my writing. I must eat again.

24 March. This Khumbu Icefall is proving to be a difficult affair to grasp. It moves. We hear its inner sounds, we sit to rest and feel ourselves ascend, and spaces open suddenly. Dangerous voids are concealed beneath.

The day has passed. Those of us remaining are demented. The Icefall shifted. Hind was absent suddenly. The stupid donkey, I thought, is gone inside. He's probably alive still. The dark crevasse contains him, upsidedown, a body wedged a hundred feet below within some black-blue, icy pit. He proved a danger to us all. My simpering companions wished to stay, to search for Hind. They were reluctant to move on. They viewed it as an omen worthy of our resignation. To me, it seemed a turn of fate which brought an increase of provisions. Hind carried only the tents, some technical gear, medical supplies. I bid him gone, God's speed, farewell. I carry the extra oxygen tank. There will be, sadly, one less with whom it must be shared. To run low on oxygen would mean to fail, or to die of madness. Certainly someday there shall be the climber who is sufficiently trained, lengthfully acclimatized, to use much less oxygen or even none.

The movements of the Icefall inspired us to rope together tightly for the remainder of its mysterious, evil formation. We heard a sound, a grisly moan, as we were leaving. It sounded like a whirring, maybe just a fracture, in the bowels of the ice.

25 March. The edges of Everest are beginning to acquire definition. It has not been unwise to hurry this day. Today we climbed a very long distance.

26 March. We have weathered night inside a shelter made of ice that we have found. It was adequately warm.

We heard an avalanche just now, a terrible, exploding sound quite far away. Many mountaineers have died beneath an avalanche. This seems the greater challenge of the Himalaya, working up between the fallings, the finding of the moments where the cornices are not quite ready to come down, the massive blocks of ice which hang above by miracles.

The end of day. We bivouac under a serac.

27 March. End of day, and as I write, my teeth are clattering. We've covered quite a distance, forced a way much higher, numb within the frigid air. I estimate minus 50 degrees centigrade. The climbing is difficult work. Upward. Again we are in a small, cave-like formation. We hunch, as though inside a refrigerator. We are stable in our bivouac tarp. Our smells waft within the enclosure. We are loathsome in appearance. My feet are cold. I am still able to feel them. I shudder if the pain should go away.

This shelter is near a high, flat ridge below what I estimate to be the final summit climb. The flat ridge is a forbidden place, grey, barren, alien. A wind blows here always. The wind attacks the ridge, attacks the climbers.

The mountain has become less technical. Tomorrow we will carry coils of the rope and not belay for a good distance, I am certain.

We are isolated, dependent solely on ourselves to be delivered from destruction. We contemplate this desolation, and we contemplate our death, because—like mountains—death is vast. I have found a person's glove. A very old glove, hard, decayed.

The entire day, Agathos didn't use his oxygen. It has seemed best and logical that I should switch my used tank for one of his. I have succeeded at the switch this night, with no particular stealth.

28 March. I write it from the 29th, because I now have strength again to lift my fingers. And the light has come again on Everest.

It was an evil day. It was a monstrous day. Yesterday. I will begin by writing of its morning. Gratchbur found Agathos all insane. Agathos had awakened caked in snow. He went outside the shelter to the ridge. Relentless wind had caused bad sleep for everyone. I say that he awoke. I mean he moved from semi-consciousness, exhaustion, to a stupor, to delirium. I then injected him with insults and with praises hoping to arouse him. I think he was suffering enteric fever. There could be no positive assurance that it was, but in the military I'd experienced a lot of people with enteric fever and knew other similar diseases which—without exception—promised only ugly, painful death. Here there'd be no cure, no miracle, no rescue. I was sure that I detected, in Agathos' frantic gaze, the violent desire to avenge his fate which, it was obvious, he was attributing to me, my leadership. So there remained one terrible alternative.

I thrust the wide end of my ice axe to the lower back of poor Agathos' head. He died.

A duty to him, and—one finally assumes—an act of kindness. In a type of prayer, I asked him for forgiveness and his understanding. I would leave him there forever.

Quickly I had second thoughts about this thing I had done. A person cannot see—or much less cause—a death without it marring him internally somehow. And yet morality may have to do perhaps with other geography.

Higher on the slopes of wind: Mt. Everest, and still in early morning. Gratchbur just decided he would die, that he would sit down by himself and there become a member of oblivion without further fight. I tried to show him sympathy. How easy, how convenient, and how painless, to expire in a soft, frozen, sleep. I stood down on his hand. My crampon pressed. I heard a bone crack. I was hoping to arouse him to his saving. Pulling back, he disengaged from both his rucksack and his oxygen and rolled away, as though a child, gently in the snow. He tumbled off the edge into eternal mist. He disappeared around a cornice which hung over the 10,000 feet to Kangshung Glacier. I experienced a strong impression of exposure. I secured his oxygen for later, should I make it back from Everest.

My parka flapped in choppy beats the whole day. My journey upward followed a line around a rock, up snow, along a short arete, until at last I reached an obstacle. It was a cliff of rock no more than thirty feet. I had no strength to do it. Bitterly I scratched at it with frozen gloves. Suddenly I thought to crawl out to the right. I noticed something like a gap, one vertically along the side, between the rock and left side of a wall of snow. I moved inside the gap and was shielded from wind. The way up was through here. At first I waited to recover strength. I chopped a platform in the ice to stand in, warmed my hands.

The passage only took exertion, not much expertise, and then the way was clear. I sank below the most exhausted state that I had known. I heard the bells of Buddhist rituals which symbolized the skillful exercise of wisdom. Wisdom always uses difficulty, or the circumstance of danger, even death, in all its expressions of success. In mind I saw the fires of a Buddhist offering, the dancers' costumes. I could smell the burning juniper, and feel the touch of silk, taste dough cakes, hear the double-reeded flutes of monks.

Vittorio Sella, the great Italian mountaineer in the Karakoram in 1909, wrote to my father of such decorative euphoria. Vittorio had experienced the mountains in a visionary way.

I stood upon the summit!

Exhausted, beaten. I stood upon the summit. Should anyone have doubt, I can describe it.

Small, and featureless, the top is flat, with tufts of snow in horizontal groupings formed by wind. Agathos, Gratchbur, Hind were, as in a spirit, with me. Carefully I checked. I slowly turned within a circle. I could see in all directions. There was no place higher. To the west was Nuptse. To the east was Makalu. And southward, was the white—the wall—of Lhotse. Far below, I saw the cwm, the Icefall, and the Khumbu Glacier.

I fixed the frozen glove I found, attached it to a rod I carried in my pack. A not too stable flag, it graced the summit.

I descended swiftly, with less caution than desired. I moved downward, over forlorn territory, through the endless wind. My coming tracks had already been erased by wind, yet I could see a few that hadn't brushed away. Twilight was upon me, light sufficient to return beyond the difficulties of the final ridge and stumble in the moonlit darkness full of starlight to the oxygen that Gratchbur sacrificed for me and then the place where old Agathos was in patient wait. I took Agathos' coat, his gloves, and other articles to fortify my wrap. I cannot know what gave me will to move. I could not feel my toes, and that disturbed my balance.

I considered discarding my oxygen so I could move a little faster, but I didn't trust myself in my exhaustion, the precious air, my being weak, elated, in a temporary madness. I could not be sure the madness would alleviate at lower elevation, even in the safety far below, beyond the Khumbu ice.

Editor's note

Could the woman with the interest in their exploits have been Tenzing Norgay's wife? Rubini's spelling of her name is Ang Lahm, whereas Norgay's wife was Ang Lahmu. The "around minus centigrade" (circo meno 50 gradi) seems to be a mistake. Was Rubini beginning at this point to lose judgment? A reader wonders what became of the body of Agathos, if it rested in the vicinity of the Hillary-Tenzing ascent.

Did Rubini experience a type of Spiritual awakening? His descent off Everest brought him into company with a lama scholar who for these many years would keep the diary from public view. Why wasn't it revealed sooner? To protect the spirit, or the legend, of fellow countryman Tenzing Norgay? Or did the lama simply not speak Italian and not realize the diary's importance until sometime later?

Translation could not be made in several places due to water smears. Sections of some pages had been torn away (presumably by accident). One paragraph had only three words which could be discerned: "ingenuo" (naive), "oppio" (opium?), and "corda" (rope). However, confirmation has been acquired that there was, indeed, a German-Italian climber by the name Gratchbur who did not return to his home in Neustetten, Germany, in 1953. There did pass through a region of Nepal, prior to the ascent of Hillary and Tenzing, an Italian "visionary" by the name of "Rubi," also called a "god man," and there does exist a diary, although obscure, which the editors were given stewardship to translate.

The diary's descriptions of the high terrains of Everest seem adequately corroborated by the books of Hunt and Hillary and Tenzing. And by virtue of the records of the Nepalese, it does appear a band of old Italians did expedition toward the Solo Khumbu for the purpose of ecology, or meditation, "at the beginning of the pre-monsoon, of '53."

It is said, in a village of the Solo Khumbu, that Rubi, suffering with bandaged feet, was killed. He lost his balance from a cane bridge while attempting to leave Everest through East Nepal.

By way of timing, it should be added, Hillary and Tenzing arrived at Namche Bazar the 25th of March, of '53. The diary was dated, "Captain Nicolino Kloche Rubini, visitor on 28 March, of 1953, atop Chomolungma. No longer does Everest seem easier to say."

The following article was scribbled out in about a day's time to fill some column space in The Climbing Art Magazine, January, 1988.

Sometimes as our lives pass before us, climbing takes on its true perspective as a reflection of countless other seemingly unrelated events, or as a consumation of those events. Even the various mischiefs of childhood hold some play upon a serious rock climb of later years. Such a thought became a theme of the following article.

Escapades of a Boy Genius

(or, The Making of a Climber)

I was about seventeen years old. Some said I was egotistical. I decided I would prove them wrong. I would go out and do the hardest crack climb ever done. It was only when I became distracted from this thought completely that I found myself, by mistake, on the hardest crack climb ever done. It was fitting that I should have to learn a lesson, that my ego would be stretched to a little wire and then snapped like a rubber band in my mind.

The Black Canyon of the Gunnison in southwestern Colorado is well known for its huge rock walls and mysterious beauty. I chose Fred Pfahler as a partner because he had just purchased a truck full of pitons. He had climbed only a few times but laughed easily and was willing to try climbing anywhere. Rich Goldstone and Bob Williams, two eastern climbers, accompanied us. To make a long story short, I wanted to climb the north Chasm View—a wall of about eighteen hundred feet. From the rim, we hiked down into the canyon via a horrid gully which led to the base of the wall. Rich and Bob, although good boulderers, had no idea how to prusik or haul and ended up sliding down ropes and burning themselves and things like that while I was leading an A4 or A5 rurp crack, belayed by Fred. It was futile, and we rappelled off. Starting to hike and climb and bushwhack back out of the canyon, some of the terrible undergrowth turned out to be poison ivy, and

Rich and Bob were unwittingly yanking it out of their way and clearly getting it all over themselves. Later, Rich's forearms looked like pizzas—the most horrible rashes I'd ever seen. But to get back to the story, as we began up the gully, I spotted a huge, very striking fissure, striking in part due to its sinisterness. It ascended a wall about like the North Face of Sentinel in Yosemite. It was terrifying to imagine myself up in there, a Crack of Doom-looking thing for about fourteen hundred feet. It was getting aggravating in the gully, and in the mid-60's I would have climbed a thousand feet to avoid hiking ten. Rich and Bob hiked out of the great abyss, leaving Fred and me to go awry if we so chose. I led up the crack, Fred content to remain second on the rope. It was already somewhat late in the day, and we soon bivouacked inside the crack on a small ledge the slant of which kept us awake a lot of the night. Cool wind blew in, out, and up the crack during the night. Through the great slit of the crack was a section of beautiful constellation. Cold, I was ready to move on as soon as it was light.

There were strange, upsidedown crawl spaces, like the Narrows on Sentinel, and there were shallow chimney structures that gave vertical, sometimes overhanging, passage. We moved higher and deeper into the unknown, wearing the skin down on Fred's elbows, back, and knees. I had done enough difficult off-width cracks and flared chimneys in Yosemite and a few hard cracks in Colorado to know that this Black Canyon climb was a real one and not just my imagination having fun. There were few places for pitons or for any sort of protection, long runouts to the point of becoming almost at ease with them. But it was near the top of the climb, when Fred no longer had eyes in his sockets, that the horror scene really began.

I must digress here and explain what I mean by not having eyes in your sockets. I speak allusively, of course, to a skull, but there is something of reality in the image. Fred was not as scared as he might have been. A relative beginner, he was trusting. I thought that he possessed spirit and courage, more so than a few experienced climbers had shown at times. Maybe it was because he was naive. He lacked a certain social sophistication, a simplicity of nature that I liked. It did not bother me that he had a tendency to sigh with a kind of crying frown-smile. As he examined the route ahead, his countenance was a mix of incredulousness, surprise, and joy, a shortness of breath, feeling both enthusiastic and faint. I knew other climbers who were alarmists, who had more fears and phobias than actually exist in the world, who not only had acrophobia but also claustrophobia and agarophobia. They had aerophobia and experienced "aeropause," a state where human function ceases. There is a condition called acromegaly, which is the sudden enlargement of hands, feet, and face while climbing. Pogonophobia is a fear of pogo sticks. But back to acrophobia. It is more than an abnormal dread of being at a great height. It is, when you are already in a high place, a fear of acrobatics. To be acrocentric is to be an egotistical acrobat. Finally, an "acrodont" is one who arrives at the summit with only sockets and no eyes. I might add still another condition called agraphia, the sudden loss of the ability to write.

There Fred was with his vacant sockets, straddling a small chockstone for a belay. The chockstone slipped down a bit in the crack, and Fred had no anchor, and I was well on my way upward into the darkest, most horrifying, part of the crack, a big flared chimney capped by an inauspicious heap of chockstones that I could not imagine anyone being able to pass. There was no protection and no way back down. About a hundred feet above Fred, the crack widened just enough that I could no longer use opposing force to wedge myself and had to start face climbing directly up the flat left wall inside the scary corridor. I was irretrievably out there, beyond any point of climbing back. The holds were getting smaller and farther apart. Suddenly there were no more holds at all. I searched wildly for a way to either side or any way down, up, or in. I glanced behind me at the other wall of the chimney. It seemed to have gotten closer again and possibly reachable. I admit that it sounds preposterous, but I literally let go with my hands and leaned backward, turning, and more or less falling over to the other wall, ending up in a horizontal position, facing downward, feet on one side, hands on the opposite, extended, gaping down into a void so fearsome that I could almost taste Fred's crying frown-smile. He glanced up at me and then quickly away. The rope hung down through the crack free and useless. I was staring at the possibility of a fall of about two hundred feet—if Fred could catch me at all while sitting on that wobbly chockstone without an anchor. The rest of the Black Canyon opened up, far below those first two hundred feet.

There is a psychoneurosis that occurs in these kinds of positions. For some, life passes before their eyes. Mine was to contemplate scenes of my early childhood which were slapping together in my mind like cards of animation. Rather than try to recall what I was thinking at that moment exactly, let me simply relate a few events of my early youth as they come to me now and which, it may become clear, played into my ultimate destiny as a horizontal wedge between two great walls, brief moments which forewarned of some ethereal, light, airy, illogical climbing predicament.

My mother, brother, and I once stopped at a grocery store to pick up a candy bar. She had earlier bought one for my brother but would get a second one for me. When the cashier asked if that would be all, I said innocently, "She has another one in her purse." My father was building the house that we lived in and was tired of having to rescue me off of the framework which I playfully conquered quite oblivious to danger. So he put me in the car to sit for a short time. Hearing a small voice say "smoke," he paid no mind. I had held the cigarette lighter in and started the engine of the car on fire. During a late drive in the country with our parents, my brother and I quietly threw my father's new tools—one by one—out the window, undetected. We watched them to see how far they would roll. One afternoon I filled a little treasure box with a whole lot of my mother's jewelry. I liked pirates and buried the treasure so deep in the earth that it was impossible for even me to find it again. When given a beautiful pearl-handled knife, I hid it by pushing it down into the mud of a small stream. No one would find it there, I thought. Nor was I able to ever again.

I remember giving a saxaphone performance in grade school. There was a large audience of parents, students, and teachers, and I was to play a duet with another saxaphonist the same age. We walked out and stood in front of the crowd and played for about two notes at which time my friend, in fright, turned and walked away. I completed the duet alone. For one with such musical promise, it was hard to believe I would let my saxaphone get run over by a car, have my parents buy a new one, and then hock it for traveling money to Yosemite.

When I was in seventh grade there was a small boy who brought me money from the cash register of his parents' restaurant, which I gladly accepted for the purchase of a fire engine which could be connected to a garden hose. I built up an enormous amount of scrap wood and cardboard between my parents' house and the neighbor's house and set it ablaze.

I tried to play golf when I was young and borrowed my father's clubs, much to his dislike. At one hole, I had to hit the ball over a lake. I made every ball from my father's bag—about thirty—plop into the lake, determined to succeed. Another day I stole six dollars off a desk in the house. With the new fortune, I set out to greet the day and happened upon a friend who offered to sell me a switchblade knife. I purchased it for the price of six dollars. A few minutes later, I encountered a friend with a new Vespa motorscooter. I asked if I could drive it. For the price of the switchblade, he would let me. Within a hundred feet, I drove straight into a garage door, the end of my ride and loss of the switchblade.

Much younger, given the present of a hammer, I am told that I carefully hammered out all of the windows of my uncle's car.

There were just as many moments of virtue and goodness as there were of folly, but it was in the nature of folly that I was now stretched between two hidden faces of rock in the heart of a Black Canyon. I worked my feet along in a backward, upward shuffle, then my hands, in increments of questionable destiny, toward the jagged obstruction of the rocks which blocked the top of the crack. The slightest bit of lichen, or sand, or moisture between my hands and the rock...I shuddered to think of such things. When I reached the blocks, I traversed sideways, first right, then left, in the same horizontal body position, until suddenly I spotted a light shining though a space between two blocks. I reached with one hand up into the space and felt around. There was a hold. Without knowing if I would fit through the space, I let my feet drop free of their wall. I squirmed, pulled, and shaped myself to the inner contours of the space, at last secure, full of pleasure, and hearing Fred's soft answers — or was I hearing his silent thoughts?

Afterward, I decided that it was not such a difficult climb. It was too deranged, too distorted, in memory to make sense out of or to be appraised beyond the several phobic confusions of a crack. I would think of it more in the context of childhood — thrown forward suddenly into a black and dangerous space.

Climbing is never just about climbing. It is about cities, terrain, people—non climbers as well as climbers. It is about the world—art, religion, politics, love, how such play into a person's experience and combine with the experience of climbing. The following poem, published in September 1989 in The Climbing Art, takes a short, reflective journey through Italy before arriving at the rock of The Grigna—a beautiful climbing area above Lecco, Italy.

Italy

*A woman comes out of
the church of Santa Maria delle Grazie,
moves into the sky as a line,
Leonardean, alone.
A trolley bus rattles down a track,
the street narrow, of brick.
In Sempione Park, everywhere
teens are fixed in a kiss.
They show their love proudly to the world.
Sforzesco Castle. A gray is in the stone,
imprint of a darker era—
but one with more erotica, more efflorescence.
What is the soil beneath the city?
A peat of bloods?*

*Violin in
a piazza.
Pleasure, opera, acqua minerale.
People blankly greet,
are consoled by a mutual coffee.
They seem in the grip of inner storms
that could in a moment
break forth with fury.
Some go mad with faith.
They exaggerate their confidence,
beautify their occupancy,
and entice you with disfigurements.*

A few of these are phantom wounds.
Daughters, as new, as dear, as time.
The bidet—
vintage Italy.

Milano endows its subjects
with great depth of feeling,
its female figures with beauty,
its men with intellectual power.
Light enters the painting from several sources,
lending it a visionary aspect—
tender in its statement of sorrow nobly endured.
A bitter, touching work.
The "grande personaggio."
A little Moses in many
(Michelangelo's visualization of an excited, inner state).
At the train station in Milano,
I am as obvious, as amorphous, as a kiss. As I walk by,
a girl has died sitting on a bench. A conductor lifts one
of her eyelids, stares into her still gaze. The steps of a
railroad car. High, intricate station dome, hiss of trains.
Italy as master, and we
briefly apprenticed to it,
oils that must be handled with regard,
yet times too self-depictive to survive.
Milano: food webs, vapors, funeral circles,
bells, relentless quarrel.
There is a certain theory of disgust,
or in other instances of courteous proffering.
Yet children are not kept from learning
that there are places such as silence.
Italy—its infinite value and unwanted lives.
The people flourish. Italy—cloyed, suggestible.

A smell of espresso.
A serenity—that aggregate of
comfort-directed instincts which compares
the amount of useful energy that can be expended
and the power of a complaint.
A street—yellow. In Italy tomatoes have a richer flavor.
Cars like rain dart through light.
But to come back to the events that are happening.
A man stands motionless against a wall.
There is no rain.
Then things cease again to happen.
He lights a cigarette.

Milano can be defiantly dirty
but has amazing resources
with which it rewards friendly attention.

Nothing can dim this city's excess of sweetness
or deny the distance that will fall
between you and it in a moment you form
an affection for one another.

There are other things that Milano
will not allow a visitor to touch,
because of the intimate nature of such things,
yet to which the great, open garden of the mind
is susceptible and will obtain nonetheless.
Love—a foregone conclusion, an inevitable result.
On a one-thousand lira note is written,
"I am looking for a wife."
A phone number is included.
In Italy love is almost a government policy.
The way an earring shines. Reading a "romanzo."

You on a steep road descend.
How do you see the world? Floating higher?
It is spring. Could this be the way it looked
at one time to Da Vinci?
We are studied, dreamlike
in the decorative sense of nonspatial art.
An exact frailty, a praise, or a cowardice.
Can a sentience of the spirit be defended?

You near. "Non ridere quando cerco di parlare"
(don't laugh when I try to speak).
I thought that I would learn Italian. While in America?
In Italy everyone is a medieval poet
trained in rhetoric,
lifted to a high pitch of feeling
by a miraculous salutation.
In America, if someone hates you
they network their hatred out.
In Italy, they speak to you in dialect.
I "importune" the language,
a matter-of-fact recital of conjugations,
a few adjectives to render mood,
employed at sub-sub-conversational pace.
A delay of incredulity

follows the moment of success.
Three semesters of study do not prepare me
for my first phone call in Italy.
The phone rings, I answer, "Pronto" (ready), and panic.
The person on the other end speaks rapidly.
To make my terror cease, I hang up.
It is difficult to believe I have hung up the phone.
The caller does not ring back.

In a delicate, ventilated train,
seduced by places where a lot of time has passed,
the air is physical desire,
but you a woman who so keeps her own counsel.
The window of the train is open to Verona —
made of lyric grace, its palaces, the churches.

Hills green with light.
A river divides the city.
There is a sense, a tension,
that our journey is to take a step
from which it will not be easy to return,
drawn in deeper, as with a dream,
farther each day into life's depth,
along light, through silky knowledge,
with wonder, hope, love, and questions.
We cross the Rubicon,
through all the fires,
through all the years which are this river of Verona
and which separate an ancient Italy from Cisalpine Gaul.

In the distance: mountains,
rock I would like to climb.
In Mestre at night, our friends — the Iovanes —
put us in separate rooms.
As I slump into a very still bed,
a plane tips, a train slants,
a girl perhaps nineteen leans slowly away into death
mysteriously on a bench in a railway station.
I lean into sleep.
All of these forms of transportation have instilled in me
an uncomfortable, kinetic floating,
as though I were still on our train,
as though it were still rushing
toward Mestre in afternoon,
rain dripping through a window of the train,
an old church seen along the rural distance,

pink and transient against some clouds.

The Iovanes are fearful for their cat
who is oblivious to danger
on a narrow ledge seven stories up.

Venice. We talk a gondolier down,
float by Goethe's house.
There are water sounds
that happen softly around an oar.
Into corridors, sunny, breezeless,
we serpentine as through a mind,
places pinched, dark, then light, a voice—
the gondolier warns another around a corner.
Streets of water. Letterings of gold.
I attempt the gender of a word.
Children play, walk in passages between houses,
hands in pockets, smile.
They seem to hide something they have done.
Cats have no particular homes in Venice.
Home is a fish smell, an alley,
a nap near the canal.
A cat doesn't have to kill an insect
that she sees on the walk in front of her.
She only has to place a paw on it
and stop it from moving for a short while.
The dialect of her meow is a kind of ciao.
Casanova's house. Mask shops—they paint them
through the window as you watch.
A ristorante in a courtyard in the back.
The sun shines into it, a tree beside our table,
a stop to eat spaghetti,
to spread formaggio,
to find a roach leg in the second course,
to hear the waiter—about age sixty—
sigh that he has found new love.
To contemplate erosion of the city
by the waves of motor boats.
Reagan is in Venice for a summit.
There is a warship in the harbor.

Light stares from the passageway of San Marco
across the bright space of the piazza.
A policeman with binoculars
on a balcony of San Marco
studies a woman who is sunning on a nearby roof.

The comparative absurdity of a machine gun.
Policemen carry them during the summit.
Thinking at this instant that I shall resonate, I
ask a policeman in Italian
when the summit will be over.
He mocks me with an English response.

The sky at night,
as a vast, oratorical silence,
is a kind of interlocutor.
It comprehends the essence, and the light,
of a conversation.
Words look for a philosophy.
To have fixed in the mind,
to be acquainted with in experience,
to be able to distinguish in the world,
a world of lost minds, a love,
a starlight, to feel
that life is moving toward a resolution,
are soft, radiant springs of night,
the emotion night
which ministers a fragrant, purple color.
Trees blow outward toward the night. Leaves,
and stars, leaves that act as the body
of a beautiful air. Leaves that follow
as the shape of a rushing current, air
full of green, blue, black, a meteoric air.

It shows one some leaves, this green full of stars,
stars in epicycle through a mind,
the stars. They show the shapes of
a rushing dream, a dream full of blue
that acts as the body.

A sky like Shakespeare, known for
its superior poetry, great delicateness,
and dramatic appropriateness,
a religious dance in its slow lights.
Within the cannon of night's plays,
I sleep, dream of you.
I weary of the intellectualism of our time—it is
cumbersome, undependable. Nothing is settled
at the summit. Night, wind, clouds merge
in desirous inclination, where one can feel
that Shelley was rescued from the sea.

One admires the scope of words,
how they stand up on a shelf
or can be typed into a circle
like a moon or an iris,
the prejudice of, say, Fellini
where, to demonstrate an artistic suffering,
darkness is given extravagant fulfillment.
In Italy, people are happy
to allegorically exist.
Stares of old men in pool halls.
A sadness, the sound of coffee makers.
There is little that is not errant,
that does not wander in quest of adventure.
Together by our love
we are apparently healthy, normal members
of the world. There are times I envision
a pleasant, domestic wife.
Yours is a fear of not remaining alone.
There are a few lonely, separate places
of the dream.

Stereotypes of Italy—male chauvinism,
dark-haired women, pasta, garlic, the Renaissance,
or wine, the Pope, Mafiosi.
But there are better things,
not necessarily beyond ordinary knowledge, just
less disclosed, a hidden courtyard, for example,
confined but open to the sky,
a place with potted flowers,
the window of the purported casa di Giulietta
where one may ponder suicide
or think of amorous adventure.
It would be a hard climb up the wall to that window
      (but worth it).
Dark, stone rooms of cathedrals are reached
by stairways that eel upward cryptlike,
then great, wide-open acrophobia—the look down
onto red roofs. One can tell by
all the churches in Verona
that there is a god.
We wash our fruit at a time-worn, stone fountain
in the market, find a park to picnic in private.
An audience of pigeons.
In Italy, no solitude should be assumed.
They compete for pieces of bread we throw,
flutter desperately into bunches.

What comes to one is at the expense of another.
Some are never fast enough.
They are used to these corporate ways,
their bodies compact, short legs,
stairs upward past the apostles
and the breaking of the bread.

Italy, in spite of the careful efforts
of its mental suffering, has a native intelligence.
But beware of the facade.
Do not believe the grandeur of the Duomo.
Italy—
somewhere
in proximity to the great and powerful,
small, infinite, confused, terrible, virtuous,
vulgar, still-to-bear the Christ Italy,
through window, from mountain,
Italy, blest as it is, disadvantaged.

Milano, where you
studied the piano with the Maestra for seven years.
You find it difficult to visit her again.
Your friends at a small factory restore pianos,
shave a surface. Your former boyfriend
takes us to a deli. I feel for him.
It would be painful to be without you.
Fragments of your voice collaborate with
the unconscious message—of love, of light.
Of walk, in Italy.

A person scrubs a dark, stone floor
of the church of Sant' Ambrogio.
Another morning, another claustrophobic,
two-person elevator. But if one feels enclosed,
there are mountains. High, rich colors. Mountains
sly, coherent, a powder-blue rock.
You don't have to go to the Dolomites.
Visit a pizzeria of Lecco,
on a shore of Lake Como,
drive upward through a forest, the road narrow.
Madonnas gaze at you from roadside niches.
Houses with wide, lovely views,
hills whose grasses softly ring the bells of cows.
Walk and climb an hour trail
to The Grigna.
The trail rises above rooftops which are

the beautiful village of Piani Resinelli.
Then up through meadows filled with flowers,
over stones, up metal ladders
that cling to cliffs,
long drops all around, uncannily weird.
Suddenly the spires of The Grigna
appear through mist,
place where Bonatti and Cassin did their first climbs.
Adrenalin. I tie into a rope
with friend Luciano Tenderini.
Up vertical rock, the side of a
three hundred-foot pillar.
The slope of the mountain
seems to drop infinitely below.

Luciano feels we need only carry the rope,
not belay.
If I were more assertive we would belay.
Up rock,
each with coils draped over a shoulder.
We pass an old piton there for sixty years,
the rock lightly rinsed by water carried by the mist.
An imagined fall is snagged by a wet hold.
Mist hides us, then moves off.
It creeps, circles, settles,
lonely, subtle, full of oxygen.
Its white air rises, crosses,
down and up the mountain, through spires,
through the space between a climbing boot and rock.
The visual references of the terrain are strange.
A feeling I am falling,
feeling of exposure, that I lean.
Rock curves among the shapes of climbers.
In a church of Verona things move this way too
in a painting by Vittorio Pisanello.
"Ho paura" (I am afraid), I whisper.
I am not as sure of myself as the Iovane cat.
In the middle of a steep wall Luciano
clips me to a piton. We begin to belay.
"Bella," Luciano describes the rock.
He smokes a pipe, watches me
as I climb below him on an edge.
I reach upward to a hold.

From the summit, rappel takes us down
to a thin grass trail at the edge of a void—

a fall into which would be
through mist. A foreign mist,
but then the sun again in vineyard bloom.
You wait for us at a place on the trail.
We return to you,
all scuffle down the ladders.
You wonder why we led you up these shelvings,
but not fatigued, not quite regretting,
never one to magnify distress. Always there are flowers
and the detail that you make of them.
We climb, I think, in ways you play piano.

Luciano, Mirella, their house
in the mountains below Piani Resinelli.
I walk out into the cool yard, into light.
Italy sings of spiritual love—
dancers beautiful, independent, and faithless.
In moods of despairing prophecy,
in misapprehensions of god, in joy, in compromise,
embittered by poverty and narrowness of religion,
crime, folly, desire, dying. In a scented melancholy
are mountain flowers.
Ironic—the defeat of man.
The sense of his achievement,
mentally dishonest as such is.
A yielding to flowers, to breezes,
a fresh-washed grass, yielding to any one of many
Italys. White walls of houses and the coral pinks.
Mirella is quiet, concerned, her father ill.
Dinner with Riccardo Cassin,
old master of the Italian mountaineers,
in shape at age seventy-nine, small in physical stature.
He tells of doing leg lifts
at night in bed before he goes to sleep.
His wife scolds him for thinking he is still young.
No pessimism, no age, no hesitation to make plans.
I feel in him an Italy,
to use the scale of his fingers
that fidget in the foreground.
Riccardo uses an Italian I do not comprehend
except in parts, for example
that I could stand to lose a little weight.
While in Italy?

Among the houses of Piani Resinelli, on a hill,
a rock is hidden in the mists,

a rock exploited by the younger climbing stars.
At the bottom of the rock, between climbs,
these young converse, smoke cigarettes.
They chuckle with the secrets of
their separate spatial practice,
this after-school place. Another joins them,
running down a path along a hedge of white stone,
past houses which have been there centuries.
One, his last name Ballerini,
leads me up a climb.
Paint, shadow, highlight.
I wonder if these younger climbers think of Italy
or how they ideate about, let's say,
the humanist scholars, the artists, frescoes,
the painting of the Last Supper — that wall
of the refectory left standing after bombings
but now fading, flaking, its image
as distant now as the archetypal church.
An art restorer stares inside an inch of it, close up,
a section upon which we, standing in the distance,
are not allowed to breathe.
The controlled temperature of a cathedral,
the cool air on a mountain rock.
You kneel down to feel a meadow,
a hill of almost endless flowers.

Lunch at Piani Resinelli.
Folk songs of men at a table outside a cafe.
A feeling of inferiority hangs over from the war,
a slight fear of reprisal
even in a moment of delicious, warm focaccia,
in an instant of clear, entrancing peace.
Uncertainty — like the flavor of blue-veined gorgonzola.
And do the young think about Italy?
A scattering of signs along their path
must connect them with a sentience,
if they receive it. A feeling one will fall.
Attraction amid opposing causes,
resistance, compliance, footing, drawn in deeper.
Religion? There is no one without a measure of
Franciscan piety, even these young, these irreverent,
whose lives are executed in what will come to seem
to them like minutes.
Verdant mountains. Light.
A pebble falls. Sound —
a moment's posthumous mystery.

Small festival in Piani Resinelli. Ghosts in light—
Riccardo as a boy in the 1920s, jubilant,
discovers light, the rock, touches ferns in cracks.
The reedy backyards, the lone havens, clouds
compounded by belltowers, terraces, and fruit.
Soft-bosomed saints lean against walls
which speak of generations of families.
A quiet stretched tight,
like strings that are strummed—distantly.
Clouds colonize the heights, a sky like little prints,
or illustrations, faces in flaring drift,
your beauty latent in a mountain,
brought out from the light.
Italy—wonderful, indolent space. Art, love,
fill the space, and names—Ubaldo, Sergio...
starry pure. I do not necessarily hold these of Italy
more holy. They are satisfactory,
not perfect enough to really lie,
more beautiful than will be misunderstood.
A moment of desolation. Mist dangles.
The corruption lies in stillness. Luciano and I, our faces,
distort, go away. We sink back
in our senses, a moment where one, as a climber,
or as a walker, shifts a little, wonders,
takes some time, feels, endures,
slowly disappears.
There are poets who squeeze love for its cynicism
and who are proud in that
nothing can reach them.
I think that I am probably very fortunate,
seen only from the highest level
of that percipient disappearance.
Yet ways we stand visible
in cities where to vanish
is probably the one chance.

At Luciano and Mirella's,
the light of love shines quickly.
You and I want to bring a quantity of formaggio
home with us. The love of light shines darkly
in the service of this princely house,
of these costumes. A small look at Italy.

Did not go to Florence, nor to Rome.
The new Italys were never built.
I think of the kindness of the Iovane family,

souls so well-risen out of the primitive swamp of man.
The pope would be charitably served
to account for this quieter culture,
a culture less intent in its search for redemption,
one which speaks perhaps
with a greater spiritual literacy
than the arch-oral societies.

There is a train
in the mountains. There is
a woman surrounded
by the grain of a flower,
a moment that is
seeded with light
but dimming,
as with a painting
that the mind studies
as though to restore.

Italy - Piani Resinelli

Photo by Pat Ament

The following fiction piece was born out of a brief period when I felt somewhat haunted and lonely and was experimenting with my writing. After countless revisions, I feel it is one of my best efforts.

In Absentia

On a train out of Varese, Italy, Polso stared through a window, outward toward passing houses. The train slanted through an afternoon, through trees, sky. Blue fell through cumulus build-ups. Sunlight seemed to travel visibly across a hill, over belltowers. The features of Polso's face exuded a vivid, preternatural intelligence. He sought anything possible to feel or with power to involve. Velocity, memory. He took every setting, every piece of art or writing, every death, to heart, a veneration that included mountains. Among his loves was rock climbing. I could comprehend Polso's own death. He would be a victim of the casual agency of suggestion.

In a room in Italy Polso sat at a table with a book of poems by Shelley opened to "Adonais," Shelley's elegy to Keats. On the table were pieces of lemon, sugar, traces of a beverage that was effervescent. An oil lamp cast light on a sheet of Polso's writing. He crumpled the page in his hands and placed it in the ashes under the grate of the fireplace. He wrote poetry that made a terrain accessible to the eye or that gave a darkness exposure to light. His reverence, the care by which he felt his way toward things, his writing, his climbing, were a type of saturated screed of his mind to which he added and subtracted. He felt often at the verge of an unexplainable something that no effort of revision could secure. Like poetry, he was finely strung, sentient. He was attracted to the English poets. Their experience, I felt, could be equated with Polso's own life. Coleridge was, from the *practical* point of view, a failure. Shelley was wild yet able to reveal, and to disturb, with a language that was exquisite. Like Wordsworth, Polso could not focus his eyes for any length away from the beautiful in nature. It was a vexation the way Polso could perceive, love, emote, while at other times appear incompatible. It was his thesis that there were places—pockets—where a wrong spirit existed, for example amid a brood of rival climbers or in a cult of teachers at a university engaged in struggles for intellectual advantage. One professor, somewhat of a misanthropist, gave climbing the disparaging description of *"death-centered."* Polso took this to be a personal attack, hostility that seemed to flow irreconcilably from those "pockets" of the world.

As Polso's friend, I found him to be goodhearted, receptive, able to weather the world's people, their bile, whatever was aroused in the way of censure or else promotion. Polso was desultory, gathering the cells of existence—climbing, poetry, and art—into a denser galaxy.

On the west coast of Italy, in evening, the green of the hills seemed for an instant to petrify his powers. There had been rain, leaving a clovery, pure air. "Corrllis," Polso said to me. He pointed to a ridge of rock that was blue. A rustle of leaves invoked a kind of soul ecstasy. What with the breeze blowing in, I did not hear everything that he was saying. I heard pieces, my first name, Corrillis, for example. The air, light, rock, and leaves held a more compelling claim on attention, something threatening picked out singly in them. I felt a wariness. There were things I did not want to hear.

Below and to the west, starlight began to shine on the Ligurian Sea.

Polso was enraptured by a genteel, very beautiful Italian woman by the name of Federica. The lean, dark-haired Federica was an easier, earthlier presence, to Polso the discovery of a rare, dustbound poetry. She possessed a nobleness, a poise of mind, along with a subtle, excited quality—as though a permanent sensation of love moved in her. Life that passed through her was illuminated, unplaced. Her mercury lived in Polso's climbing, in the flint-coarse rock, in his walking among the woodland spirits. She and he tabulated incidents in their lives. She sipped espresso, an assembly of anti-heroine, genius, and higher spirit, extremely feminine, prodigal, attainable—betrayed in part by the vocabulary that was hers.

"You will take me to climb?" Her voice was lovely and low.

Black, glistening hair nearly to her waist, soft skin, a trace of wine on her breath, she was entrancing, a scent of something wild, like berries, the afternoon dilating. She pronounced her name,

Federica Akillanna Spasia. The name held sounds of death and space. She was voluptuous before him. His cult struggle as a climber rose up—not to answer desire or be spirited away, he thought. But then he was sitting near her arms, and her hands. She spoke to him, to her advantage, and he to her in return with all of the courtesy that one exhibits when in a foreign land.

Polso, as seen by her, was the lusty markets, the spring, the drifts, and cataracts. She felt a softness in the image of his pillowy boyhood. He was the babble of the men of the village whose youth and loves lay lost. Some men outside a tavern joined in a laugh against themselves.

In a series of vagabond attempts, Polso and Federica visited France, Wales, places in Italy where an impulsive fancy led them. A night in London, he waltzed with her beneath starlight on the brick of a narrow, rain-puddled street, a necklace of lightnings, air tinged with nectar.

Through him she could begin to feel that the mountains were beautiful and that they possessed a spirit.

Polso believed Federica to be the abler being, yet the two had excellent influence on one another—Polso learning a clearness from Federica and Federica gaining in her sense of grace from the climbing, or from the poetry, of Polso.

Polso and I climbed in rain on a wall of green-black rock that rose against the side of a valley. The rock was partially covered in flora that grew vine-like from cracks. We belayed each other as though in a running—blind, upward, drops of water thrown down and hitting the charred-looking rock. We followed what appeared to be a light—visible somewhere above, behind the rain. It was a kind of dreaming for holds, hands reaching upward into the splashing light toward new holds. We brushed rotting leaves off holds. Boot rubber scraped against the rock. Polso verbalized the route, sentences thrust down at me like stones kicked loose by his steps. We arrived through the rain to where the rock ended on a slope of grass, a strange, secret agora, or island, delicately cool. A sheep had reached that place. Polso seemed perturbed by its still, ghoulish dumbness. There was a feeling that we had gone through the rock rather than up it, that we had captured the internal form of the rock. The peculiar light we had been climbing toward seemed to come now from below, in the valley.

Polso exuded the energy of the rock, harpylike, a portrait of the spatial gestalt of the rocks. He sought the creative storm—dissolution and then wholeness, as in music, tension and then release. He did a few climbs alone, with no rope or protection. A small dampness of his fingers, an over-extending, and he would have been dead. He believed that life had to take chances, perhaps fall through air at a height of manic frenzy. Polso had no ground plans. He borrowed from his own life, with no sinking fund built up to pay off the final debt. He had ideas about professions to which he might one day commit himself. People gaped into his eyes, at his sinewy, emaciated form. It would have been boorish for an on-looker to ask Polso what an adventure was like. There could be no transfer of reality to them, for there was no supporting framework. He moved, always, into the center of the power, upward on rock, his eyes a touch-light rush of adrenalin, breathless at the instant joy—at the shudder—of eluding danger.

Occasionally, when there were no more holds, he was forced to retreat, to leave a climb, and then to dream, to walk in an intensity, distrustful of what he had been unable to complete.

There were times when Polso and Federica fell away quietly from each other. In melancholia he would leave for a short while, and away from the mountains. During one such spell, Polso and I visited Spezia—in Shelley's time a refuge for artists on the west coast of Italy. The air was wet. From a hill, Polso stared outward to the space of the sea. A storm drove us from that place. When the sun came out, we were pointed toward—covenanted again with—the mountains.

Polso moved with new preparations. He spoke about different textures of blue in a sky, about a tincture of red tapering downward in a cloud. Yellow alongside blue, he pointed out, enhanced one another, whereas if yellow light interacted over blue each was cancelled. I chided him: "Tell me, Polso, nefarious gnome, where life flows." He replied, "The beauty of the path is the locus of its meaning, and paths vanish—as does a season."

A fast electric train carried us through England. In London, in an outdoor market, Polso contemplated buying a ten-foot long, skinny eel. In the National Gallery in London, Polso disappeared into a room full of Rembrandts. He esteemed Da Vinci's "cartoon." We visited the dead in Westminster Abbey. Gazing at the commemorative plaque for Auden, Polso recited a line of Auden's, "...the shadow cast across your lives by mountains." Polso was impassioned by the dark Abbey, its dream kingdom for the weary traveler, the tall, stained-glass windows, altars made of gold, tombs of queens, tombs of artists. What had those individuals achieved? A heritage? A vision of God? Something too personal?

Or pained? Polso thought that his writing should become as quiet, as accepting, as Mary Queen of Scots at the moment the axe was poised to fall on her. The Abbey was a place for Polso's thoughts to practice their sharp, unorthodox arts.

A young, saintlike girl of remarkable beauty in the chapel of Saint Martin's in the Fields listened to several musicians perform Bach. She closed her eyes, as though eroticizing the music to assist a private prayer. What did Polso seek in her? Something kind, sane, miraculous?

Polso's religion was to feel faith but at the same time be attracted to a spaceless, godless death. For him the madness of the world needed a place of annihilation, as urgently as it did of healing. Beginning a climb, Polso whimsically uttered the Biblical prophet's words, "In vain is salvation hoped for from the hills, and from the multitude of mountains." Yet did he hope.

Federica went about her life more quietly, in less reflection. Proper, continent, she conveyed her love of Polso softly. It was in Italy that Polso had taken his name, a gift of Federica. She radiated love for the day, for Polso, for anything that was a source of life—a saucepan, a path, a tree, a hand. As they sat at a table, she touched the back of one of Polso's hands. Her low alluring voice, her interior energy, were the embodiment—the concealed substance—of a metaphysical poem. She found the unusual, existential figure of Polso pleasing, their measure of time together undetermined as yet but holding a character of anticipation. They lowered their guards with a superior intricacy, joying in their association—as it hit home to them. I felt grateful for the stroke of fortune that had brought them to each other.

In England, an evening following some glasses of beer, we walked along a street. Polso noticed a wall of brick with insets between the bricks that invited climbing. "The foe-beset climber shall now attempt the great wall," he began. "What are its secrets? Ahh, the sweet sigh of danger's awakening breath. Give me thy holds! And thy churls." He pulled himself up the wall by his fingertips, concluding, "Else shall I squander...(the edge of a brick pulled away, he fell back to earth, his body immune to pain) ...the privilege of life." In the underground, near a track, a tuba-clarinet combo played. Polso related to some hoboes under a bridge near Charing Cross Station. Later he took on the visage of a lord, asking for caviar. A woman from Long Island, New York, described London to Polso, "There's a lat goin' on."

Polso was considerate, placing slings, creatively clipping carabiners to flakes in the rock, taking pains to provide protection for me with the rope. A climbing day resonated with quiet, granular sounds of his shoes. He defied difficult rock, and I was absorbed into competent participation. The rock was like pottery, warm out of a kiln. He could be caught in the depth of a handhold, as though staring into a memory or at a distant place he saw in the hold where something might go wrong, or had gone wrong, deep in a life. For Polso climbing was like literature. It hurled him through incarnations, through mind gardens.

From the summit, we made several rappels down a different wall than we had climbed — less demanding than the ascent yet exhilarating and lively. As we reached the ground, Polso drew into himself as though hesitant to display some vacuous triumph. Seeing that I was still a little bit electrified by the challenges of the climb, he mused that we had assumed we could pursue radical enlightenment without experiencing anything radical.

For a couple of weeks, Polso lost his desire for climbing. He worked at poetry. In his writing he hoped for any influence of a genius such as Shakespeare's, characterized by a kind and melting heart. Yet Polso's mood did not suit poetry either. He spent a day with Federica, but it seemed to be uncertain time. As they departed from me and walked together, I heard Polso say to her, "You were going to tell me something, if you remember." Conscious that he was looking at her, she turned her eyes away beautifully. There was a significance to be found even in a simple statement. Their walk led them among trees with old, stone houses in ruin, places his imagination stored up as settings for poetry. The two moved through a solitude of flowers, along an ancient, elm-bordered road, a sunlight familiar to Federica.

Growth, I thought, depended upon our link with beautiful environments: the mountains, or poetry, the quiet, listening Federica. I wished them affectionate regard and left for Florence for a few days.

It pleased Federica that there was no interpretation of harm when she would briefly distance herself from Polso. She applied herself to innocent, daily toil, expending a portion of her energies for example in a garden where she cultivated flowers. Daylit yellow walls rose up to the red tiles of roofs. A breeze lifted limbs. His image appeared in her thoughts, exceeded in intenseness only by her regard for it, and all the while letting him go. Perhaps one strong-felt gift of Federica was this releasing service she added to his nature.

When I returned, Polso was quiet. It was as though he had experienced some kind of disillusionment about himself. He lacked an energy that existed when he felt that Federica was fully in his life. Perhaps the difficulty was no more than her moving back a little into her own life. As she had appeared out of the light, it was natural—inevitable—that she would disappear again at least in small, temporary ways. While giving Polso a sense of belonging, she also affirmed in him his isolation. Federica was not an absolute. She was mature in her own independence, and in her solitude, for which he was somewhat prepared. It eased his pain that, in knowing Federica, some degree of elegance would always visit his thoughts. It seemed ironic that such things should occur here in this land of renaissance and place of the Renaissance which so bade that a human being find within him or herself the resources of an individual fulfillment.

Polso wrote because what he felt inside ordered matters so. His poetry was objectivist, presenting an object, scene, person, along with specific, nongeneric items, clothes, housewares, all forming, without force, a memoir of somewhere he had never altogether been. The writing was made of "contacts" with people, the progress of a love affair, agitation, nights, a mountain, a fabulous meadow at night where he began to dream the spiritual life-history of a supreme moment leading out ahead of others. Sometimes the voice of the poetry was confused. Wicked tramps moved from dream to meal. Faces had disturbing glances. There was a fine distinction between the real and the feared. Often a woman was near the center of his images, a woman whose demeanor lent moving power. Much that he expressed was what he felt that he lacked, as though by practicing such things artistically he obtained them in some way.

In a restaurant he ordered a drink—something dark—and was nourished by simply sitting, absent from climbing, poetry, or longing. He rationed the drink, extracting from each sip a flavor, glancing out a window, observing Italy, streets, buildings, faces, their friendliness, or haste. He touched his glass, let it sit. An edge of it reflected light from a window. He ran his fingers around the light, then along small cracks in the surface of the table. Even a drink and a surface had their whorls, their copse, mists trying to open to a life.

What seemed to others a pin-point world took on, for Polso, size. As he gazed into a sweep of sky, one could only guess as to the dimensions of the abstraction. Conversation he and I engaged in went all right, yet he began to deny himself an instinct for questioning. It was a quality that had become easy for him, habitual, to a degree that I paid it no mind. Disturbingly, it was gone. I wanted to get him back, so to speak, to feel the language that before had communicated his activity and his imagination. Perhaps to expose his heart to a friend would have been to acknowledge things that were in his heart.

At a table by a street in Paris, Polso watched a game of chess played by two old men. He was attracted to its dense, referential poetry. We separated for a few days again. In Italy, at a hotel where I told him I would end up, I received a postcard:

> *"Corrllis, It is dark tonight. I sit alone, immure myself in rooms. My visit to Marseille was warm. I thank you for the quantity of Trebbiano, drank it slowly. Federica. I continue for her always. Flowers, sky. It soon will be that you and I must climb. At times the paths of friends must separate, but later they will join. The transience. Take care of life, take notice, be observant of the starlight in the mountains. Shall I keep my name?* — Polso"

I remembered the tenderness Polso expressed in the Abbey, the way he stared at the plaques as though to commune with the names inscribed on them.

Polso and I attempted to climb the Cima di Voci ("Summit of Voices"), a face of rock above the village of L'Aiuola ("the Flowerbed"). We ascended without conversation, feeling our way in an intricate balance up slightly less than vertical rock. The rock was damp. An edge of one of my boots found a small hold that, as I stood on it, gave off a vapor of fog. The weather was strange, more cloudy but less cold than it had been. We were hampered by a certain fear of the weather but continued. There was something beautiful in our minds that had not yet been answered with a reality. Green smoke rose up from the village. Voices could be heard far below, men in a quarrel over drinking scores. Even on the mountain there was a scent of fruit rind. There were tomato, grape, and bread smells of a market. Cows stood in a field. A train creaked by the foot of L'Aiuola. A lake lower than L'Aiuola, in a valley, was purest blue. Wind gusted in some trees.

I could see two or three young Italian women on a street. From our distance above, I could see that one of them wore a white dress. I could imagine meeting, perhaps falling in love with, one of them, someday, thoughts that changed to the stone: the Voci offering itself to our hands.

Downdraughts off the rock blew into my sleeves. Polso's mind attempted—as minds do—to expand forever, his eyes cast upward by life's learning of itself. The turbulence of the clouds emphasized for him the open space of the sky. He was invulnerable. But the word life could become the word death, depending upon the placing of the accent—in madman parlance. The wind left the mountain. I wondered if conditions were going to improve or if this calm foreshadowed a storm.

A terrible ruckus of cracking rock suddenly exploded downward: Polso was swept away.

There was no hurry to descend to him. I had little urge to exploit my state of mind—inexplicably composed. My parasympathetic nervous system reacted with force to compensate for the horror of the reality. Polso was alive, at the window of a train, his elbow on a pub table of England, Polso unremoved, conversant, exasperated by some episode of his own thought. In climbing, Polso was level, equable, deliberate. Returning to a familiar climbing area, Polso courted a mood. He watched for a proper sun, or a shade of light, which mirrored an experience of his past.

Polso and I visited the cathedral of Notre-Dame, perhaps the theater of France's greatest climbing. He explained that in the fifteenth century Quasimodo traversed among the structure's gargoyle walls. Quasimodo moved up the facade, under concealment of night, to a particular sculpture, to the seasonal deities of Ceres and Proserpine, to admire them or speak at them, as though they were alive. Priests stepped from their chambers by candlelight to glimpse, near the starlight of an upper window, their sentinel who guarded the flower rows. Quasimodo gave himself to the beneficence of the cathedral, as did Polso, I thought, give himself to the sanctuary of the mountains. No longer inhabited by Quasimodo, the cathedral of Notre-Dame had an inanimacy. The dragons perched solemnly in their places. The supernatural griffins frowned. Even the saints gazed downward as though into a void.

Ice melted from high reaches of the mountain, and water fell luminously. Sunlight glanced inward through passages of the sky. Pink, transparent clouds moved like lobsters toward my position.

I began to descend, in a direction slightly away from the line of Polso's fall, toward colors of the spectrum that were like a veil to another life.

They gathered his pieces and placed them in a crate for shipping to a grave in America. His two connections with that grave were that he lived as a boy in those hills, and this was a cemetery near his closest relative, Zolis Kazmirez, an alcoholic stepfather. I had met Kazmirez and felt a great bitterness in his soul. Now Polso's death aroused in him a clear, intelligent remorse. He arranged a burial. I was interested in attending but decided to remain in Europe and return in spring, as Polso and I had planned to do at the outset of our trip. The man wrote to me of the burial, describing a breeze that was warm, the sunlight. He spoke of some cumulus that must have belonged to a range of mountains where Polso had left a spirit. It was as though Kazmirez could sense my denial of Polso's death and wanted to pull me toward it by planting in me these impressions. I began to feel Polso's helplessness at the instant of his fall. I could see through his eyes, tumbling as though in a clothes dryer, wrapped in a swirling destruction of blocks. I could see L'Aiuola, the young women in the streets.

One tries to minimize any presence within lines of potential rockfall. One detests the ugly sound of rockfall as it eases loose from a frail, hanging position overhead. At first it is a tiny, distant sound, then rapidly increases in amplitude like a freight train. Bullets of rock fire down, within and around the central mass. There is the effluvium—an odor of burnt rock where the falling shapes have left their touch. Before such a rockfall, a wind will leave. Afterward the mountains will seem quiet or be covered with benevolent light.

Our rope was silently, easily, severed. Had this disjoining not occurred I would have been dragged with Polso. This was the sort of ironic fussing that was slow to exorcise itself from a mind. I tended to think that in three days a stone would roll away from a sepulchre. Polso would emerge bleary-eyed, private. He would speak about people who snore in climbing huts or would tell about a particular woman who thought his backside was his best side. He would ask what was haunted about the mountains, would insist that the dead were haunted by us. I could see him in Greece, tasting a piece of soft, white feta.

I wondered what I had been to Polso, our dealings, adventures, the travels, celebrations. It was his jeu d'esprit that each of us was eventually a lost, haphazard wretch to whom the flake of life had given hope. I could see him within the bright, white-gray, stone sanctuary of La Madeleine at Vezelay, France. The European continent had been, for about a year, home for us both. We had aligned ourselves with its railroads, cobble streets, languages, and rock aretes that rose upward into Polso colors. Italy was a reddish dark. Polso had greeted its people, like a poet sought amnesty among them. They had included him, fed him, served as his friends. The shadowing geography of the earth, sun moving down behind a blowing tree, uncertainty, the mummified air.... Evening was infiltrated by voices, along with scents of dinner. I sought the vibrations of lower lands, the sea—its fragrance blown toward me, a kind of answer to act as intermediary between my romanticism and the life ahead.

Rock surfaces opened, closed in contradictory ingressions into one another. In fact, climbing was no more pernicious than life, religion, or love. Polso had read to me from the last stanza of that elegy of Shelley's, "The massy earth and sphered skies are riven!/ I am borne darkly, fearfully afar!/ Whilst, burning through the inmost veil of heaven,/ The soul of Adonais, like a star,/ Beacons...." Like rockfall, these words fell on me from a hidden place.

Rain began like photons, drops of light, a chain of excitation falling, then decaying in a colorless black.

I remembered with amusement how Federica filled Polso with lifeblood one day when he was careworn and acting like a hollow void. Her intrinsic, outward-looking light directed itself at his frame of mind, and he was, in a second, left wearing an embarrassed elation. Her solid, felicitous remarks, and his footing a little shaky, they balanced their way through such occasions. She pushed aside a part of the shadow of the world, and they laughed and argued with equivalent energy. Upon coming to such accord, they hastened away to some secluded room where, I pretended to know, he kissed her and approached her and she hesitatingly assented to other mysterious and soft forms of touch or sexual enticement, attracting and persuading each other, all shared with appropriate awakeness, arrangement, and delay, entering each other's souls, enjoined in a darkness, attention as well as imagination enhanced, showing—as much as admissible—their truth.

Love, I thought, was a strange training ground for oblivion. I passed people whose eyes, it seemed, reached out with a tenderness to meet—or perhaps cause—the tenderness of others. I wished that I could go into such beings, place in them a love of my own. Behind such faces were the mountains, was the massive sea, where Polso and Federica's spirits flowed.

I felt a certain renewal yet also dissatisfaction in bidding these few months goodbye. I met with Federica briefly, felt her gentleness, her purity and intent. As we parted, her sudden absence instilled in me once more a twinge of euphoric horror. Life had its senses of temporality, but also the enveloping force of a mystical experience. Every hour rearranged the patterns of human association and created new environments. Qualities of awareness happened deeply in our lives, sometimes almost without our knowing. I tried to feel the impact of what my environment was saying. Friends and I were connected, folding over and through each other, feeling life's mix of beauty and inhospitableness, and feeling love — that central point which underlay all. To look at rock and find that it should contain such suggestion was a notion expressed by light which fell now on small, inland mountains, Polso mountains, impresario of their secret entertainments.

What seemed might be my final visit to Yosemite, in early June of 1990, inspired the following somewhat wandering nostalgia.

This article was accepted for publication in Rock 'N Ice Magazine, 1991.

Climb To Safety

(in case of flash flood)

Outside the Tuolumne store I am greeted by John Bachar and several other climbers who are listening to a naughty rap music at tourist-scattering volume. A beautiful, cool air blows over and up the granite of Tuolumne. Sections of the rock where there is glacier polish are brown and sparkle. My companions, Steve Brawley and Tim Schultz, are eager to have rock climbing challenges placed in front of them, to have me lead or let them lead climbs up domes with heart jumping runouts above protection. Climbing to Steve and Tim, both twenty-three, is urgent. When you are that age you are a god. You must do everything, and you can do everything. You will never die.

Bryce Wilson joins us from Los Angeles, not a great climber but very much of a character. We hoist him up what we can, a heap with a harness and a pair of sticky shoes. We don't care if we are held back, if the compensation is to be amused. The Bachar-Yerian route can wait, until another life. Bryce is tolerant of the indignities he suffers at our hands.

We find a campsite not far east of Tioga Lake, add spices to some Dinty Moore stew, then stand out among alpine tufts in starlight. I recall my first visit to Yosemite at age seventeen with Royal Robbins, our first night spent open in a Tuolumne meadow where Royal pointed out constellations—Orion, Cassiopeia.... I still feel how much power radiated from that man, as he stirred from his sleeping bag the next dew-covered morning, ready to climb in his valley.

Steve, Tim, Bryce, and I search sunlight for miraculous, small, granite knobs we guide our toes and fingers to. The route offers a look outward, a sweep of high country, or down at the river and the long, wide meadows, a vista that reaches in many directions. Sight is broader, more expansive, more in focus, than through any camera lens. You see with unbelievable depth of field, then in close at the bright, perfect stone as you locate a knob or you notice the runout and feel a little rush of the willies. Years of your life pass by you as fast as that thrill.

Our plan is to do the short drive back and forth between Tuolumne and Yosemite Valley, to play in both locations for a total of about a week. I wanted to come back to Yosemite one more time, make a little review, have a few final reflections, return to favorite climbs, once more run myself out up a wicked, vertical handcrack, and feel that type of fear, that sense of survival, which is unleashed sometimes almost in the form of a supernatural power. I wanted to drive through the two hundred-foot tall sequoia, stare into clear, dark, green pools of the Merced, study the greens of lichen, see old friends, bump into a few of them casually as I did always. Would I chance upon any of those women I thought each different year were the answer to my problems, who rubbed lotion on my Tuolumne sunburns or let me play the piano for them in the small chapel in Sentinel Meadow, or who I loved closely *in* Sentinel Meadow under stars?

Bryce has brought enough sleeping bags to stack into a Sealy Posturepedic. Tuolumne is disturbed by Tim's snore. In the middle of the night, I hear Steve yell at him, "Shut up." And then more emphatically, "Shut up." It is not easy to reconcile that such sounds should bray from one who climbs with so much sensitivity, who radiates almost a reverence toward the unfoldings of a route.

Steve is a materialist — buys a car, a motorcycle, and, with his last fifty, a #3 "Friend." A climbing store salesman tries to sell him a couple of artificial climbing wall holds, but Steve comes with us to collect real ones. He squeezes knobs as though each were the next delightsome, irrational purchase.

Steve leads upward, anchors to an old, rotted sling. I correct the situation when he brings me up. I must monitor these children. We share a lone, golf ball-size knob which is the largest in four hundred feet.

Steve tells of when he worked as a waiter, how he took a woman's unfinished steak to wrap up for her, forgot, and instead threw it in the garbage, then remembered, retrieved it from the garbage, and gave it to her.

The four of us have breakfast one morning at the very small Tioga Lodge where a ludicrous deer head is mounted on a wall and two fore-hooves are bent upward in "L"s as hatracks. The store sells postcards of redwoods, paper probably made from redwoods. I overhear a tourist explain that the reason Ansel Adams was such a good photographer was that he had a special camera.

Royal's heartless stare. In 1967 when I did the West Face of Sentinel in about twelve hours, going up two pitches in late afternoon, spending the night, and finishing the wall the next day with light left to have done those first two pitches, Royal stated that—because there had been a bivouac—it had to be considered a two day ascent. When I led the first 5.11 in Yosemite in '66, a resentful local went up later and pried a loose block from the crack so that a handjam was created where there had been space only for the tips of fingers. The route could then be downrated to 5.10 c or d. This sometimes was how an outsider was welcomed.

Driving into Yosemite Valley I think of Howard Nemerov's line about trees, "To be a giant and keep quiet about it." There is a parade of RVs the inhabitants of which peek out upon occasion to view Yosemite Falls or El Capitan, excited as they observe Texas Flake which they believe has moved. What does it mean these days to climb El Capitan? Climbers throw their excrement off it packaged in paper bags which, as you stroll up along the base of the wall, you encounter. People hang glide from the summit. People parachute El Cap. Paraplegics prusik it. Likely it has been soloed by a two-headed woman. Royal would argue that this could not rightfully be considered a solo ascent.

There is a type of climber who must do the Shield route on El Cap. They form a line at the foot of the wall. They are unfeeling and have no good connection with other people—like the climber in the '60s who, fearing a bust, swallowed his complete supply of acid and for years afterward struggled to make sense of what people were saying in conversation. These Shield climbers are quiet and speak only the language of the Shield. They file off the summit as perpetually as they lash themselves to the initial pitch. Rurp cracks up there are now bong cracks, three inches wide, a millimeter deep. Ting ting ting. You will always see a few tiny, red parkas high on the Shield. The people on the Shield never move. Rather they are replaced.

In the Camp 4 parking lot, a climber (just off the Shield) stands at his open VW bus door, hash pipe in one hand, beer in the other. He is in a trance, stares at a point on the ground, unbelieving of what he has climbed—or else he has been hit hard on the head by one of those poop bags.

I savor my July heat ascent of the Nose of El Cap in '67. It was the ninth or tenth ascent of the route. I was nineteen and, to my parents' dismay, hocked my saxaphone to afford the trip. My partner, Tom Ruwitch, was seventeen and had only climbed a few months. El Cap is a wonderful rock school and a genuine dose of consciousness, probably worth a music career.

I tour boulder problems I put up in Camp 4 in the late '60s after spaghetti dinners, a night or two when the rock and I seemed divinely acquainted. The climbing world has no memory of these routes. Only spaghetti has survived. I walk around the problems, recall their footwork, their gymnastics, the strength and mind I gave to them at the peak of my physical form, a soft-spoken Barry Bates sometimes bouldering with me. To touch these holds is poignant, taking me back to my obscure, personal season of pushing extremes. Brought to recollection also are strange freight train wanderings to and from Yosemite, freight cars, starlight, alfalfa, or desert, when I carried within myself a fresh fix (or new anticipation) of Yosemite. All the years of climbing now condense into one acute, perplexing emotion you can intimate to the outside world only by being for a moment intensely quiet and looking away as though toward a sacred, distant place.

We walk slowly up the trail toward El Cap. Something swishes down hard into the trees. Someone try to bungee jump from the Shield?

Leading the Sacherer Cracker without the right gear, spoiling for a fall, I think of its author Frank Sacherer, killed in the Alps, his bold leads during Yosemite's golden age, how he led quickly so as to conserve energy and moved upward, often without protection, to the terror of his friends. I think of Chuck Pratt who made lasting impressions on all of our minds with his mastery of cracks, his and Royal's and Frost's committing ascents, the walls of El Cap done without helicopters standing ready, without fixed ropes, without double-bolt rappel anchors leading down the wall. Memory conjures obscure countenances: a fellow I spoke with in Yosemite in the '60s who a day or two later drowned crossing a river in King's Canyon, climbers each with their own amazing spark of ability who after a few months or years left Yosemite for good, who were too hurt by its changes or who did everything they desired to, or simply the day of their inspiration was gone, or through drugs or loneliness they lost that extra will to care about climbing anymore. One imagines Salathe and Steck up there during the first ascent of Sentinel. Harding, after a lot of wine, made plans with anyone for a new route on El Cap and then in the morning would not remember having ever talked to you. Mort Hemple playing his guitar among the trees. TM Herbert, in the visage of an Indian, talking about shooting the squaws in the rumps with flaming arrows. Jim Bridwell transcending an impossible off-width crack. The feeble, frightened whimpers of Chris Fredericks as he led a pitch. Pete Williamson hanging dead on his rope after drowning at the crest of Bridalveil Falls. Jim Madsen falling three thousand feet from the summit of El Cap while trying in a storm to rappel dry coats to Pratt and Fredericks. Layton Kor stemming wide, his pants split into two separate halves. Tom Frost's cheerful, truthful smile. Chouinard, living off tourist leftovers in the cafeteria of Yosemite Lodge while hammering rurps into their early shapes. Mark Clemens, Peter Haan, Lauria, Breashears, Barber, Beck, Jardine, Erickson.... I recall a comment by my friend Tom Higgins, "There comes a time when climbing memories far outnumber climbing prospects." Yet his mentor Kamps leading 5.11s at age sixty. The crack that now is eating my hands asks for quick upward movement, like when Rearick sat on a rattlesnake. What a den of thieves and visionaries those times all were, some of us now priests and others cynical drunks who once were forebearers of a climbing magic and antecedent to the procession. We have not all heeded E.E. Cummings' counsel:

> *You shall above all things be glad and young.*
> *For if you're young, whatever life you wear*
> *it will become you; and if you are glad*
> *whatever's living will yourself become.*

I discover that one of my haunts, the lounge of Yosemite Lodge, is no more, determined to be too much of a hangout for chess players, musicians, and that smelly genus—the wet, tired climber. I recall playing the piano there, Breashears listening, and recall chess with Bachar and Bev Johnson, and Bachar's sunglasses that had a tiny red light behind each lens that blinked on and off—a great tool of interchange when sitting among unsuspecting tourists.

My gaze is diverted to a long, slender blonde who, upon closer study, I detect is a man. To be counted among the new order, it seems, one must be of dubious gender. Although I have never had hair on my face or my chest, I seem to be clearly a male.

All of these are thoughts that subtly interrupt the long sequence of the Sacherer Cracker. What this route needs is someone focused, a Ron Kauk, who concentrates on the texture of the rock more than on how he composes and paints his life. I hear the horns of a traffic jam along the road in the forest. I worry whether the young girl I have hired in Colorado is looking after my cat. For a moment the slightly dangerous runout seems ironic and to reflect the whole subtle, spiritual genocide of Yosemite. I envision myself fall and my head glance fatally over the rock.

I think of that loner Bachar who has liked me and led me up a few climbs. At the top of New Dimensions, just where the crux of the route occurs, I was belayed by Bachar but took note of what it might feel to be there solo, as had he been, a thought which comes from where William James calls the "chill periphery." The largest challenge for Bachar is to keep such a spirit in any semblance of abeyance. The climbing of today's stars is so convincing that it requires courage to see them justly and that their vital chapters will be where our previous story shall get much of its light. I see the names Pete Croft and Werner Braun on the Yosemite rescue list. How can people live in the valley for such long periods and not die of its lack of culture? Is it that climbing and nature completely satisfy their needs? Somehow they must move about, in and around the surface view of Yosemite and find an unusual intimacy with places no others go. Pete Croft is a miracle upon the scene, with his calm traditionalism, an ability that shoots holes in Alan Watt's thesis that you have to hangdog and sport siege in order to approach the new thresholds of skill.

Starting in the later '60s, climbing has been for me gradually less overt and more interior, less brute expression and more susceptibility. I learn that I know. Each technique is a memory of experience. In a certain coincidence, hands find holds. Footwork has a charisma that is a driving joy. I have thirty-two years of climbing. Now half my former fitness, I better understand climbing's science of forces and benefit, as I succumb to obsolescence, from a certain ascendancy (excuse the pun), a compulsion for establishing myself in improved positions of balance to reduce the difficulties a bit. Growing weaker inspires a new, different artistry. I try also to look deeper at my friends and more appreciatively at the physical environment and rock than could I when I was so breezy, buoyant, and strong.

How does one appraise his climbing, or his life? For me it is as I appraise my writing. I am jeered and revered. A person from Wisconsin wrote that my prose is "...Boulder's answer to Little Debbie's Peanut Butter Bars" (a defense, or a critique?), while the anthologies of best climbing writings (Games Climbers Play, Mirrors in The Cliffs, etc.) include me more than almost any other writer. The poet laureate of America recently wrote to me, of my poetry, "I am moved by your work, by its good feeling and its kindness." Yet some of my moments still have their haphax legomenons. I didn't wait to be a polished writer before I exasperated people with almost the bulk of what one should ever say. Some see me walk down the street, and they think, "He must live in some clinic." Then I am invited to give a poetry reading at a university or be the guest speaker at England's national mountaineering conference. My friend John Gill has told me to take pride in having an enigmatic persona. Because I live in me, I know who I am at my best. It is a tendency to assume other people should see that. Probably foremost of my faults is presumption. I have assumed also that the bad should not be seen.

Something Tom Frost has tried to teach me is to accept criticism of myself in good earnest. Life as it progresses takes on the nature of a mystical event, as though before you were half conscious and now you are coming to. Those whose life work seemed to be to cut you down turn out to appear reasonably discriminating. But most have tired out on the effort, now that you are more open to it. I see the text of my life as a very good one. It would have made a great difference for the better, perhaps, had there been a clearer destination in mind and had the images I pursued been less often at the stage—which ought to be preliminary—of impressions. One certainty: I have more friends that I love than I have people who hated me. Some of it is a love based on a far away instant of days. Part of the pain of existence is that, even with good friends, there is a process of separation. Sometimes it happens quickly, or else slowly the while that you know each other. You go your ways, disassociate softly, for simple lack of time or as vicissitudes carry you to another place. Pratt would still recognize Roper and Royal. Does Schmidz ever think about Madsen? Where do I stand anymore with Higgins, in light of his daughter and wife and work?

I think, it was because Royal loved us all that he was so hard on us. I think no, he was latently egotistical and self-righteous, a grim reaper, bearing his dark plague. I return to the first thought.

Royal, who Frost refers to in retrospect as "the chief," truly was our spiritual leader, bearing our highest integrity.

Climbing is a lot easier than to sustain the better thought about anyone. But with Robbins the task is not so difficult.

Bryce must return home. Steve, Tim, and I act as tourists, visit the gift shop for postcards and teddybears. We take snapshots of high, towering granite. I must say to Galen Rowell that Yosemite is not a good test of one's photographic genius. Frankly, in Yosemite, any grandpa could raise his instamatic into the air, click the shutter, and it would be a masterpiece. A few of those grandpas get their cameras slapped out of their hands by bears who have not given them a written release.

The day before Higgins is to drive from Oakland to join us in Tuolumne, it snows. I phone and leave a message on his answering machine: "I guess you are reprieved of having to see me. After finishing the second pitch of Nerve Wrack Point the blackest cloud you have ever seen descended on us. Interesting way to end my final trip to Tuolumne. Farewell, my friend."

I have two parts of myself. One is a feeling that we will look back on this life as some trivial moment or some brief mission wherein we were to gain knowledge. Another part of me, perhaps the atheist, conceives salvation as the largeness of our experience of life. While I try to look beyond life, I value every detail of what here may be all. At dark a coyote ambles down the edge of a road. The coyote is soaked, for an instant confused, blinded by headlights, a moment of indecision and cold, rain dripping from its mouth. This wild, lost, lovely creature at last gets into the trees, stops, looks back, safe in the respirable green from people who move about with their laughter and contempt and their lights. There are times when you feel the pain of animals, how they struggle and suffer. You think that they didn't ask to be born, and that they deserve what dignity you can pay them. Somehow I feel that I asked to be born.

Mild flooding chases us to a rented tent in Curry Village, an expensive and lazy act. People with umbrellas tip-toe between deep puddles toward restrooms. John Muir and Teddy Roosevelt are among them. Steve and Tim write in their journals. They do not view me as the broken memory of a climber I feel I am becoming. To them I am one who has made climbing his help, who has made it a resource of stability, something to grasp, studies in how to hold on, how to protect, a sanity of technique. I guess that is what climbing is, when you are going nowhere with it, some-

thing refined, something that keeps telling you that you are someone—when in your heart it is the tendency to believe that you are
no one. It is a mystical knowledge that can't be told to anyone if
they are not there yet. But what you can tell friends is each slant of
your foot, and your respect for them. I think specifically of delicate, beautiful, Shannon Wade. Shannon is one of those giants who
keeps quiet about it. Above all things she is young and glad. She
looks freshly at climbing, certain that climbing is going somewhere, like her, budding, that climbing is not falling apart.

Breakfast at Curry Village, then we take showers. The showers
in Yosemite have never changed. They burn you and then freeze
you, and then burn you. We drive by El Cap. Sunlight touches it in
a way that reminds me there will always be a solitary, beautiful
wall behind the circus. I notice a dark green pool of the Merced,
the same sun on it as a day I caught a fish each cast. Unexpectedly
trembly as I begin to lead Outer Limits, I think of the nearby route
The Twilight Zone, Pratt leading it in the '60s with no protection.
He was the epitome of when the mind is tuned aright.

Tim says goodbye. He will head west to Santa Barbara to meet
a woman. Tears which touch so many parts of me well visibly in
his eyes, from having to part and to leave the soul-perplexing,
colossal visuals of Yosemite cloud and rock. Steve and I begin our
drive east, through Tonopah, Nevada ("home of the muckers"),
and into the sage of desert. I can feel the strangely moving power,
a superior power, of those doorways of youth, how climbing stole
into our hearts and was seen as a life that would be continuous with
our own, a climbing sometimes absurdly alarmingly hilarious, and
those hallowed few instances when the very deepest meanings
stood indelible to our minds.

About the Author

Pat Ament was born in northwest Denver in 1946. When his father took a position at the University of Colorado in Boulder, Pat found himself living at the foot of beautiful mountain terrain and the huge, intriguing flatiron rocks. He quickly recognized these rocks as his calling in life and became a young member of the handful of seriously devoted climbers in the area in the late '50s and early '60s. In the company of Royal Robbins, Layton Kor, Chuck Pratt, John Gill, Tom Higgins, and others, he later became one of the best, most creative rock climbers in the country. He pioneered hundreds of first ascents and first free ascents and accomplished the first routes of a 5.11 grade in both Colorado and Yosemite. As a university gymnast in the later '60s, he was second only to John Gill as a boulderer. Many of his boulder problems on Flagstaff and in Yosemite remain as testpieces today. He demonstrated his ability for longer climbs as well, with the 4th ascent of The Diamond as a highschool senior (1964) and as a teenager doing the 10th ascent of the nose of El Capitan. Other big wall routes included the West Face of Sentinel and the Black Canyon's Chasm View. He has continued to be an active rock climber and is widely acknowledged as one of the most insightful, sensitive climbing instructors in the world. As Tom Frost writes, "Pat has been a climber with a powerful idealism and a mentor influencing some of the outstanding climbers of three generations."

Five or six of Pat's climbing essays have appeared in international anthologies of best climbing writings. He is author of four books of essays, six guidebooks, a biography of John Gill, and approaching a hundred articles published in various climbing magazines and journals. He founded and edited nine issues of a small literary publication on climbing and has lectured widely in the United States. He was twice guest speaker for the National British Mountaineering Conference. A filmmaker, he won the 1984 "Best Spirit" award at Telluride's Mountainfilm festival and won a $1500 prize from the University of Geneva, Switzerland. He won an award for his artwork from the University Of Colorado where he also received a degree in creative writing. He studied poetry at the graduate level with Reg Saner and others, has guest taught writing at the University of Colorado, and has been invited to give university poetry readings.

Pat bouldering on Flagstaff in the late 60's

About the Author

Access: It's everybody's concern

the ACCESS FUND

THE ACCESS FUND, a national, non-profit climbers organization, is at the forefront of efforts to preserve climbing access throughout the United States and is supported both by individual climbers and the climbing industry. The Access Fund defends your climbing by providing financing for land acquisitions, support facilities and improvements, funding scientific studies of environmentally sound climbing practices, publishing educational materials promoting low-impact climbing, and providing start-up money, free legal counsel and organizational resources to local climbers' coalitions.

Climbers can help preserve access by being responsible users of climbing areas. Here are some practical ways to support climbing:

- **COMMIT TO "LEAVING NO TRACE."** Pick up litter around campgrounds and the crags. Let your actions inspire others.

- **DISPOSE OF HUMAN WASTE PROPERLY.** Use toilets whenever possible. If none are available, choose a spot at least 50 meters from any water source. Dig at hole 6 inches (15 cm) deep, and bury your waste in it. Pack out toilet paper in a "Zip-Lock"-type bag.

- **UTILIZE EXISTING TRAILS.** Avoid cutting switchbacks and trampling vegetation.

- **USE DISCRETION AND BE CONSERVATIVE WHEN PLACING BOLTS** and other "fixed" protection. Camouflage all anchors with rock-colored paint. Use chains for rappel stations, or leave rock-colored webbing.

- **RESPECT RESTRICTIONS** that protect natural resources and cultural artifacts (e.g. Indian rock art). Refrain from using power drills in wilderness areas. Agree not to chisel or sculpt holds in rock on public lands – no other practice so seriously threatens the sport.

- **PARK IN DESIGNATED AREAS,** not in undevelpoed, vegetated areas. Carpool to the crags!

- **MAINTAIN A LOW PROFILE.** Other people have the same right to undisturbed enjoyment of the area.

- **RESPECT PRIVATE PROPERTY.** Don't trespass in order to climb.

- **JOIN OR FORM A GROUP** to deal with access issues in your area. Consider clean-ups, trail building or maintenance, or other "goodwill" projects.

- **JOIN THE ACCESS FUND.** To become a member, simply make a donation (tax-deductable) of any amount. Only by working together can we preserve the diverse American climbing experience.

The Access Fund. We're working to keep you climbing.

The Access Fund, P.O. Box 67A25, Los Angeles, CA 90067